The Autumn Assembly Book

The Autumn Assembly Book

REDVERS BRANDLING

STANLEY
THORNES

First published in 1993 in Great Britain by
Simon & Schuster Education

Reprinted in 1995 by
Stanley Thornes (Publishers) Ltd
Ellenborough House
Wellington Street
CHELTENHAM GL50 1YD
England

A catalogue record for this book is available from the British Library.

ISBN 0 7487 2379 X

Set in 11/13pt Times by
Columns Design and Production
Services Ltd, Reading
Printed in Great Britain by
T. J. Press (Padstow) Ltd, Padstow, Cornwall

Contents

Acknowledgements

I am, as always, grateful to the staff and children of Dewhurst St Mary School, Cheshunt. They have been a receptive audience for all of the material in this book, and a source of both inspiration and information with their own presentations.

The material supplied to schools from Save the Children and the Christian Education Movement has been of great value. Of the many anthologies referred to, *Folk Tales of India* and *Folk Tales of the World* (both published by Sterling) have been especially valuable.

It should also be mentioned that some of the stories in this book have been used, heard and re-adapted several times in assemblies. In consequence their original sources are not remembered and if this has unwittingly caused the infringement of copyright, the author apologises and will correct this omission in future editions, if notified.

Introduction

'Effective assembly occasions take a great deal of time to prepare.'[1]

'Assemblies must contain a sense of expectancy, a willingness to co-operate, some unity between those present by reason of shared experiences or common values.'[2]

'In achieving this meaningful act . . . other means . . . are valid . . . stories and readings; dance and drama; prayer/meditations; creative silence; songs/hymns/music; sacred/secular readings; artefacts and natural materials; children's contributions; visual aids.'[3]

[1] *Themes for Assembly* S Brimer, Blackie and Son
[2] *First School Religious Education* T and G Copley, SCM Press
[3] *Collective Worship in Hertfordshire*, Guidance for schools.

These quotations effectively reinforce what all those who take even an occasional assembly already know. Apart from its being mandatory, a daily requirement, the primary school assembly should at all times be well presented, thoughtful, reflective, and involve the children. For ever-increasingly busy Heads and teachers it is therefore an extremely demanding task.

This book seeks to provide constructive, practical help for a complete autumn term of assemblies.

It begins with a series of fifteen ready-made assemblies for each month – September, October, November, December. These assemblies are 'instant' in that they provide an introduction, story, suggested hymn and prayer. They also, however, contain sections on 'Information for the teacher' and 'National Curriculum cross-curricular reference.' The use of these will hopefully enhance each assembly and, as with any ready-made material, reflection and preparation beforehand add enormously to its potential.

The second section in the book contains a number of class assemblies. Once again these are prepared in a detailed manner – aims, materials required, calendar location, numbers involved, preparation, information, presentation – and contain a variety of play-scripts. The latter are reproduced in large print so that they can be used for photocopying and group involvement.

Section C contains an anniversary, fact, fancy or anecdote for every day in the autumn term. Many of these are ideal starting material for other assemblies and interspersed with them are notes referring to ready-made assemblies elsewhere in the book. Where this is the case, links of ideas or themes offer further expansion possibilities.

For teachers who do not wish to use the assemblies chronologically and prefer a thematic approach, then Sections D and E aim to help in this context. The former groups assemblies into popular primary school themes – *animals, concern, courage,* etc. Section E links the assemblies via a sources context – *folk, true, religious, original,* etc.

Section F acknowledges that many teachers now feel that assembly material should be linked to other areas of the National Curriculum. This is done here by identifying other National Curriculum subjects and linking assemblies to them where appropriate.

The final section in the book provides details of resources.

Redvers Brandling

Section A
Complete assemblies

September

1 She's new

Introduction

Starting a new school in a new place where you don't know anybody can be quite frightening. How would you help somebody in this situation?

Story

Jayna was . . . well . . . just miserable.

During August she had, unexpectedly, come from India to live in England. Now, having moved into her new home just one week ago, here she was in a new school. She knew nobody, could hardly understand the way all the other children talked, and felt cold all the time. She was miserable.

Mrs Gillespie, the teacher, tried to help. She put Jayna in one of the friendliest groups and asked everybody to help her settle in. But, there were thirty-four other children in the class and everybody seemed so *busy* with their own affairs and their own friends. In fact, in every spare moment the other children on Jayna's table seemed to be working away at something between them, but when Jayna tried to get a look at it someone always seemed to get in her way. She felt terribly left out.

The days passed with agonising slowness. Eventually it was Friday. Soon she could escape this awful place for two whole days.

When Jayna went into the classroom that Friday morning she could sense a different atmosphere. Everybody seemed to be waiting for something. Mrs Gillespie spoke.

'Is it ready now, Julie?'

'Yes miss,' replied one of the girls on Jayna's table. 'Come on Wayne, let's carry it out.'

Julie and Wayne carried a roll of thick card out to the front. Jayna realised it was what the group had been working on since Tuesday – if only they'd let her help, after all she was quite a good painter.

'Right,' said Mrs Gillespie. 'Open it out.'

Slowly Wayne and Julie unrolled the card and, as they did so, all the other children clapped. As more of the card came into view Jayna began to feel her eyes tingle and her tummy grow strangely tight. Soon the whole card was stretched out across the front of the room.

'WELCOME, JAYNA' it said in big letters, and underneath were the names of everybody in the class.

Now Jayna knew why . . . but what could she . . . it was . . . suddenly Jayna didn't feel miserable at all.

Information for the teacher

This is a familiar theme in many schools in September. One 9-year-old child captured its essence in the following words:

> A loving arm
> Shelters me
> From any harm.
>
> The shelteredness
> Of kindness
> Flows around me.

Hymn suggestion

Come and Praise Vol 2 'It's a new day' No 106

Prayer

Let us think this morning about being a good friend. Let us try always to treat others as we would like them to treat us. Let us try to really understand what we mean by the word 'welcome'.

National Curriculum cross-curricular reference

This work could be linked with a 'new' theme in Science (Environmental Education) – new growth, baby humans and animals, needs of new things, etc.

Geography can be pursued by examining the background of every child in the class – where their home is, how far it is from school, drawing routes and plans, hazards to be watched for, etc.

2 Being different

Introduction

This is one of those stories which, when you listen to it, you think: 'Oh I would never have behaved like that'. But . . . could you be sure?

Story

Life was going on very much as usual on Planet Zemon. The space shuttles arrived from different galaxies, the living blocks maintained the same temperature as always, the automatic self-drive cars swayed round each other to get to their programmed destinations. Then, he arrived.

'I've never seen anything like him,' said RBT 1.

'Nor me,' answered WRBT 2.

'Where has he come from?'

'I've heard that somehow or other he's been transported through a time zone from a place called Earth.'

'Have you noticed the clothes he wears – disgusting – not at all like our all-in-one plastic coverings.'

'And food too – he doesn't like the computerised meal tablet bank. Keeps saying he'd like real bread and cornflakes, and something called chips.'

'Worst of all, when he was in the programmed environment he even seemed worried about that.'

'When they pressed "Summer Scene" to come up on the screen he said it wasn't the same as real trees and real grass.'

'Did you know that MEGA R had asked robots to invite this . . . person . . . into their homes? Well, I'm not going to.'

'Nor me. Indeed, if it was up to me I'd suspend him on Time Warp Island.'

'Yes, certainly get him away from us because he's . . . well . . . he's . . .'

'I know what you mean. We don't want him here. He's . . .

'Different! That's what he is – different!'

'That's right. We don't want anybody who's different here.'

Information for the teacher

1 This may be a useful early-in-the-school-year assembly as, in the hands of a sensitive teacher, the material could be used to lead on to discussion of intolerance, in any of the many areas in which it is shown.

2 A useful calendar reference here might be the story of Roger Crab, who died on 11th September, 1680.

Crab was a soldier in Cromwell's army and then a successful business man in the field of selling hats. He suddenly decided to give up his affluent lifestyle; he gave away his shop and all his money and went to live in a wooden hut. Because he had chosen to be 'different' he was accused of being a wizard and tortured many times.

Hymn suggestion

Come and Praise Vol 1 'Black and white' No 67

Prayer

Lord, teach us to enjoy and appreciate the differences in people which make our world so interesting and varied. Help us always to be tolerant and understanding and never mean and narrow-minded. Help us to be a contented part of the family of man. Amen.

National Curriculum cross-curricular reference

The theme of 'Difference' can be followed up in many historical contexts – slavery, American Indians, waifs and strays in nineteenth-century London, etc.

3 Keeping a diary

Introduction

One of the most famous events ever to happen in this country took place in September, 1666. This was the Great Fire of London – but how do we know so much about it?

Story

The Great Fire of London destroyed two-thirds of the city: 13,200 houses, 430 streets and 89 churches. The fire could be seen from forty miles round the capital.

The reason we know so many details about the fire is that two men who were alive at the time kept diaries in which they described the dramatic events. The names of these two people were John Evelyn and Samuel Pepys.

Other famous people who have kept diaries were Queen Victoria and Captain Scott. Queen Victoria started completing diaries when she was 13 years old and continued throughout her life. But for Captain Scott's diary we would know very little about his brave but unsuccessful attempt to lead the first party of men ever to reach the South Pole. His diary was found after his death.

Another diary which was found after its owner's death was that of Anne Frank. In it, a young girl describes what it was like to have to hide for months and months in the upstairs room of a house during the Second World War.

Here are some notes from a girl's diary of today:

4th September: Back to school. I sit next to Aliya. Our new teacher's name is Miss Hawksmith.

5th September: My turn to have a go on the computer, it was great. Brownies tonight.

6th September: Mum's birthday. Wayne and I bought her a cake and it's not yuk. She says she's twenty-one, but we know she's not.

Perhaps one of the most interesting things about diaries is that they focus our attention on time – what we did yesterday, and the day before, last week and last month. When we think more carefully about time we realise how precious it is. Once it has gone we can never get it back again. How important it is therefore never to waste time.

Information for the teacher

1 Some actual quotes from Pepys' diary might be useful:
   2nd September: '. . . walked to the Tower and there I did see the houses at that end of the bridge all on fire . . .'
   4th September: '. . . the sky looks all on fire in the night . . .'
   7th September: '. . . saw all the towne burned and a miserable sight of St Paul's church burned, and Fleet Street.'
2 Still one of the very best books of prayers is *Prayers of Life* by

Michel Quoist, (Gill and Macmillan). Although not specifically for children these prayers have an ageless appeal. In this particular context 'Lord I have time' is a most evocative and appropriate example.

3 'Don't waste time' is a philosophy which has been pursued in various poems and sayings. It might be useful to have some Biblical comment here:

'Be most careful how you conduct yourselves, like sensible men, not simpletons. Use the present opportunity to the full . . . do not be fools.' (Ephesians 5, 15–17)

Hymn suggestion

Come and Praise Vol 1 'Travel on' No 42

Prayer

Dear God, Help us to use time wisely. Help us to learn from the past and make the most of the present. Teach us to value our time at school so that we can prepare for the future. Amen.

National Curriculum cross-curricular reference

The most obvious links here are with History and Science. Diaries offer a contrast between local/recent and global/distant events and opinions. Other diaries which might be followed up in the latter context could be James Boswell's and John Wesley's.

'Time' in the scientific context offers plenty of practical possibilities in both Key Stages 1 and 2, with obvious links to Maths. The diary aspect also incorporates many facets of English National Curriculum requirements.

4   A Maori heroine

Introduction

Sometimes we have to do something without any time to think. This morning's story is about someone who had to do just that – and how her courage and quick thinking saved many lives.

Story

'We're on the rocks!'

The desperate cry came from a seaman on the deck of the small sailing ship. The 'Delaware' had sailed all the way from England to New Zealand in 1863. There had been no problems until 3rd September when the ship was caught in a terrible storm near Pepin's Island.

There, fighting the tremendous waves and howling wind, all seemed lost when the 'Delaware' struck submerged rocks a hundred yards off the coast.

The crunching, tearing sound of the rocks on the ship's bottom sent a chill of fear through Captain Baldwin. He knew it was only a matter of time before the sea pounded them to pieces.

'Sir, sir – on the shore – look!'

Another cry rang out from the deck. Baldwin peered through the spray to the distant beach. A group of Maoris stood there.

'Quick, get a line ready to throw,' shouted the captain. 'And you,' he went on to a passenger who he knew could speak the Maori language, 'tell them what we're doing.'

Try as they might however the crew couldn't get the safety line to reach the Maoris on shore. Time was running out fast. Then Huria Matenga, one of the Maori women, plunged into the raging seas and swam to a large rock near the ship.

'Now throw it,' she yelled above the turmoil.

This time the line reached her easily. Then, diving back into the sea, she swam once again to the shore. There the waiting Maoris pulled the line, and the heavy safety rope attached to it. In a few seconds the rope was made fast to a rock and the seamen began to swing along it to safety.

Soon, all but one of the crew were safe. Then the rope snapped and a huge wave swept the last man away. But for Huria's bravery nobody would have survived.

Information for the teacher

1 The 'Delaware' was 241 tons and made the passage from England under the command of Captain Robert Baldwin.
2 Huria Matenga was a very important Maori woman, being the chiefteness of three tribes.
3 In recognition of their bravery Huria and the other Maoris were presented with watches and sums of money by the people of Nelson, on New Zealand's South Island.

4 This story could be added to a collection of 'heroes and heroines', the point being made to the children that such brave people come in all shapes, sizes, ages, etc.

Hymn suggestion

Come and Praise Vol 1 'Somebody greater' No 5

Prayer

Dear God, Let us give thanks for all those people, now and in the past, whose only thought has been to help others, regardless of the danger to themselves. Give us the strength of character to help other people wherever and whenever we can. Amen.

National Curriculum cross-curricular reference

There are possibilities for Science here, particularly in a 'sinking/floating' context with regard to ships; History (developments of safer ships, improved methods of rescue and survival, etc.) and Geography (New Zealand, where it is, how to get there, climate, etc.) can be involved.

Physical Education in a swimming context can be used and Technology might be served by some work with ropes.

5   Laurence

Introduction

Is your name Laurence? Do you know anybody called Laurence? The following story would be of very great interest to anybody with this name, but apart from that, it is a tale of great courage about a man we can all admire.

Story

The Roman Emperor Valerian stroked his chin and looked at the officers surrounding him.

'These Christians have got to be stamped out,' he said. 'They are a danger to the empire.'

'I agree, your majesty,' said a tall, sly-looking minister. 'But whilst we are getting rid of them why don't we make it profitable at the same time?'

'What do you mean by that?' snapped the Emperor.

'Well, why don't we command that deacon fellow – Laurence – to collect and bring to you all the wealth of all the Christian churches in Rome?'

Valerian sat silently. In his mind's eye he could already see the caskets of jewels and money this order would bring in. 'Not a bad idea at all,' he thought to himself. His face gave none of his thoughts away. Leaning forward he spoke brusquely.

'See to it.'

So in the year 258 AD the order went out. Laurence, a young deacon of the Christian church, was ordered to collect and bring the churches' treasure to the Emperor's palace.

A few days later he stood in the courtyard of the palace. The imperial officer whose idea it had all been came out to meet him.

'What are all these people doing with you?' asked the officer. 'Are they all carrying treasure?'

'None of them is carrying anything,' replied Laurence. 'You asked to receive the treasure of the Christian church – here it is.'

The officer looked puzzled, and then Laurence waved his hand at the huge crowd gathered behind him. 'It is the people of the Christian church who are its greatest treasure!'

For a minute there was a stunned silence, and then the officer screamed to the guards to arrest Laurence. For his 'insulting behaviour' in response to the Emperor's orders, Laurence was sentenced to death.

Like many other martyrs, however, Laurence became an inspiration to others who followed him. He was declared a Saint of the Church and finally, in 312 AD, the Roman Emperor became a Christian and the persecution of Christians throughout the Roman Empire stopped.

Information for the teacher

1 St Laurence's feast day is 10th August and there are about two hundred and fifty churches in England dedicated to him.
2 The Escorial Palace in Madrid, built in 1563, stands on the site of a monastery dedicated to St Laurence who was thought to have been born in Spain.
3 September link – getting to know new children's names.

Hymn suggestion

Come and Praise Vol 1 'The Building Song' No 61

Prayer

Dear God, Let us give thanks for those people whose courage acts as an inspiration to us all. Amen.

National Curriculum cross-curricular reference

Time and location could form links with History and Geography here. The time of the Roman Empire, and locations of Rome and Madrid could be investigated. There is also scope for drama and writing in connection with this story.

6 I'm sorry

Introduction

The title for this morning's story is 'I'm sorry.' These are two words which we often find very difficult to say!

Story

Hephaestus was believed by ancient people to be the god of fire, and also the god who looked after the month of September. Here is one of the stories about him.

Hephaestus was the son of Zeus and Hera. One day, after an argument between his parents, Hephaestus took the side of his mother. Zeus was so furious he threw his son out of Olympus, the home of the gods.

'I'm falling!' cried Hephaestus as he plunged through space for a whole day and night. Then, with a cry of pain, he landed on earth near Mount Etna. He was badly hurt, but when he recovered he used the great fires of the volcano to make things.

He built two golden robots who followed him around everywhere. Then, after a great deal of work, he made a spectacular golden throne.

'Now,' thought the still-dissatisfied Hephaestus, 'I'm going to get my own back on my mother. She let my father ban me from Olympus and she's never looked for me or tried to get me back. I'm going to send her this golden throne as a present.'

Now the point about this throne was that, although it looked magnificent, it was really a trap. Hidden springs meant that anybody who sat down in it would be trapped.

Eventually the throne reached Hera.

'It's wonderful,' she muttered to her servants, and sat down on the beautiful seat. Immediately hidden springs clamped shut over her. She couldn't move.

Try as they might the other gods couldn't release Hera. It was decided that the only thing to do was to bring Hephaestus back from earth. The gods knew it would be difficult to get him back so they tried all sorts of tricks, and flattery and false invitations.

Finally the god of wine, Bacchus, tricked Hephaestus into drinking some of his wine, and while the god of fire was sleeping he was taken back to Olympus.

Once there and awake again, he saw his mother trapped in the golden throne. As he did so, all his feelings of wanting to hurt her left him.

'I'm so terribly sorry,' he said, and rushed forward to release his mother from the cruel, hidden springs.

After that Zeus, Hera and Hephaestus were just delighted to be together again. All their disagreements were forgotten. But now Hephaestus had another home and soon he returned to earth to work again in his great forge at Mount Etna.

Information for the teacher

1 Although this is a very spectacular story of contrite behaviour, it could be compared with other examples within the children's own experience. A useful source for stories like this is *The Myths of Greece and Rome* by H A Guerber (Harrap).

2 The Romans believed that September, because of its associations, was the month in which fires, volcanic eruptions and earthquakes were most likely to happen. This provides a good opportunity for a link with the Great Fire of London in 1666.

Hymn suggestion

Come and Praise Vol 1 'Light up the Fire' No 55

Prayer

Dear God, We are thinking this morning about how hard it is sometimes to say 'I'm sorry'. This is particularly difficult when somebody has done something unkind or hurtful to us first.

Give us the strength to realise that it is much better to be at peace with each other. Please help us in this way. Amen.

National Curriculum cross-curricular reference

A lot of English work in speaking, writing and drama can be developed from the telling of spectacular stories. History, through tales of the ancient gods to the Fire of London, provides many varied sources.

Scientific work could also be obviously linked to a fire theme.

7 Marooned

Introduction

If you had to go, alone, to a desert island, what things would you take with you? What would you miss most? What would worry you most? The following story might make you think about these things.

Story

A few clothes, a knife, a hatchet, a kettle, a Bible – Alexander Selkirk looked at these things as the hot sun shone down on him. They were now all he had in the world.

An hour or two earlier he had been a member of the crew of the sailing ship 'Cinque Ports'. Then, after the captain had accused him of preparing to lead a mutiny, he had been rowed ashore to the tiny, lonely Pacific island of Juan Fernandez, and left on his own.

The date was September, 1704. Questions burned through Alexander's head. How would he live? Was he here for ever? Would he never see another human being again? Feeling himself beginning to panic the lonely sailor decided to explore the island.

Some time later he knew that there were no other humans on the island, but that there was plenty of material to build a hut. Working hard, he spent the next few days building one hut to live in and another for storage and cooking. He became an expert fisherman and hunter very quickly and lived on fish and goat meat. He used the goat skins for clothes.

As time went on Alexander's shoes wore out so he ran along the stones on the beach until his feet were as hard and tough as leather. Every day he read the Bible. The thing it took him longest to get used to was the loneliness. Then he had an idea.

The island was full of wild cats – what if he tamed them? Starting by giving them food he soon made friends of these savage creatures. When he had done so, dozens of them came to lie on his bed at night and keep him company.

For four years and four months Alexander Selkirk lived like this, and then, on 1st February 1709, a British ship anchored offshore and a landing party found the abandoned sailor. Alexander was fantastically excited to have been found but it had been so long since he had spoken to anybody that it took him days to be able to speak properly again.

Eventually the ship, 'Duke', which had found Alexander, got back to London. Within a very short time his story made him famous. A writer called Daniel Defoe heard of Alexander's adventures and decided to write a book based on them. You may have read this book, and you will certainly have heard of it. It is called *Robinson Crusoe*.

Information for the teacher

1 Juan Fernandez is a remote island in the South Pacific.
2 Defoe was a prolific writer who published his own newspaper. *Robinson Crusoe* was written when he was 58 and its profits helped him to face debt and ill health.
3 Selkirk was 27 when he was marooned.
4 He returned to sea and in 1720 set sail on a voyage to Africa. He never returned, dying of yellow fever on the voyage.

Hymn suggestion

Come and Praise Vol 2 'Give us hope Lord' No 87

Prayer

Dear God, Give us the courage, strength and skill to deal with the unexpected in our lives. Help us to make the most of the abilities you have given us and teach us to value everything we learn. Amen.

National Curriculum cross-curricular reference

History and Geography both have links with themes like voyages and ships of the past; social conditions relating to seamen; the Pacific.

There is also scope for CDT in a 'self sufficiency' theme. English work could include some reading from *Robinson Crusoe*.

8 This month

Introduction

Every month of the year has interesting things about it. These can be very different. Let's think about September.

This month

September is an important month for everybody who works in a school! For children and grown-ups it is the beginning of the school year, a time of new classes and changes of teacher. It is a time of beginnings.

Outside of school it is a time of both beginnings and endings. Summer is ending and nature is getting ready for winter. The leaves on some trees are changing colour and others are already falling to the ground. Hedges and bushes have berries on them and birds who spend the winter here feast on these and grow fat in readiness for the hard times when it is cold and there is little food. People enjoy berries too, and blackberries collected from hedges make delicious jam.

There is a lot of activity in the sky with swallows and martins gathering in great flocks and preparing to fly off to warmer countries. If you get the chance to see any squirrels this month try and look closely at their tails. These are now getting thick and bushy so that their owners can wrap them round their bodies for extra warmth.

September is a month when we remember some great events of the past – the Great Fire of London (1666); the opening of Britain's first railway (1830); the start of the Second World War (1939).

Information for the teacher

1 As a follow-up to this assembly some outside observation would be helpful. Depending on localities and opportunities, the following natural things might be observed: horse chestnuts usually offer the

first and most dramatic change in the colour of their leaves; leaves will already be falling from limes, and acorns from oaks.

Animals are getting their winter coats; birds are congregating; mushrooms and other fungi are beginning to appear; spiders can be found around the school buildings; daddy longlegs (craneflies) are prolific.

2 Two particularly appropriate September poems for use with primary children are: 'Friends' by Elizabeth Jennings, and 'Back to School' by John Walsh.

Hymn suggestion

Come and Praise Vol 1 'Autumn Days' No 4

Prayer

Dear God, Help us to use all our senses to appreciate the lovely month of September. Help us to be a good friend now that we are back at school. Help us to enjoy work and play during our school days.

National Curriculum cross-curricular reference

The colours of September make it a good month for Art, and for making collages of natural materials. Science and Environmental Education are obvious links with this assembly material and possibly a 'change' theme extending this. The latter is also a useful Religious Education theme at this time of the year.

9 *What do we see?*

Introduction

Elizabeth once said to her mother: 'I like bananas because it's only when you peel off the skin that you find out how good they are inside.'

In some ways this is a bit like people. What they look like on the outside doesn't tell us about the qualities they have 'inside' – and sometimes they are just waiting to show these qualities. This morning's story is about just such a person.

Story

The sun beat down fiercely on the old town of Capernaum. Clouds of dust rose round the feet of travellers as they made their way through the great gate of the town. The man who sat at the gate mopped his sweating brow as he arranged the piles of money on a table in front of him.

Two men stood outside the gate and watched him.

'No wonder he looks miserable.'

'Nobody will have anything to do with him, will they?'

'Well – do you blame them? There he is, a Jew, collecting taxes from his own people to give to the Romans!'

'Yes, and I bet some of the money goes into his pocket too.'

As the two men talked, others handed over their taxes to Matthew, for that was the tax collector's name. As they did so they muttered harsh and unkind things to him. He said nothing in return, just keeping his eyes down and fingering the piles of money on the dust-covered table. It was then that Matthew heard another voice.

'Matthew, come and follow me and we will teach men about a better life.'

Looking up, Matthew saw Jesus standing in front of him. He had already heard something of this man. Could Jesus really be asking him, Matthew the hated tax collector, to join him in his wonderful work? In a second the mean, closed-in look disappeared from Matthew's face. With a smile he stepped round his table of money.

'I'm ready, Master,' he said, 'and thank you.'

Information for the teacher

1 September 21st is St Matthew's Day.
2 There is more about the recruitment of the first disciples in Matthew 4. A list of all twelve disciples can be found in Mark 3, 16–19.
3 A useful class follow-up to this story might be to ask individual children to name what they think others in the class do well. Teacher tact is necessary here and the scope should be as wide-ranging as possible.

Hymn suggestion

Come and Praise Vol 2 'Sad, puzzled eyes' No 74

Prayer

Dear God, Help us to see the good in people. Let us not pay too much attention to appearances, but to try and get to know what qualities people around us have.

Let us pray that we may be given the strength and wisdom to show, and use, our good qualities. Amen.

National Curriculum cross-curricular reference

Religious Education – this work could be extended to examine the qualities of the disciples. Going even further, discuss what makes a good follower. How do people show their true selves? To whom do we turn for help in time of need?

10 A woman at sea

Introduction

In times past there have been quite a few jobs which men thought women couldn't do – until a woman proved them wrong! This morning's story starts with a little girl who was just not interested in the things girls were supposed to be interested in.

Story

'Victoria, where have you been? You're filthy!'

'It's all right, Mum, I've just been taking that old car engine to bits.'

Victoria Drummond's mother looked at the grease and oil which covered her daughter's hands. No matter how she tried she could never keep her little girl away from engines, tools, oil and grease.

'I don't know what we're going to do with you,' gasped Mrs Drummond.

But Victoria certainly knew what she wanted to do with herself. As she grew older she became even more interested in engines and when she was nineteen she began to study to become a ship's engineer.

When she passed her exams she was the first woman ever to qualify for this job. But there were still difficulties . . .

'We don't want a woman on our ship.'

'She'll never be able to do all that heavy work.'

'Women are unlucky on ships.'

These were the sort of comments Victoria heard, but she wouldn't give up. Finally she got a job on a ship going from England to Australia, and she proved to be so good that ships were always glad to have her after this.

During this time the Second World War broke out and one day Victoria was in the engine room of a ship when it was hit by a bomb from an enemy plane. For a time it seemed as if the ship might sink, so Victoria ordered all the men from the engine room to go on deck where they would be safer. They didn't want to leave her, but she insisted.

More damage took place to the ship and Victoria fought with the controls as broken pipes fired jets of scalding steam all round her. So hot was the steam that she would have been blinded or very badly burned if she had got in its way. Finally she managed to get things under control and the enemy planes flew away. Her engine room crew rushed back to help their chief.

'You're safe, Miss Drummond,' they cheered.

'But for you the ship would have gone down!'

'That's enough of that,' said the modest Victoria. 'Come on now – back to work.'

But more people were to hear of Victoria's bravery. When the ship docked back in England she was invited to Buckingham Palace to receive a medal from the king. Many people were pleased that a little girl had once loved engines as her favourite toys!

Information for the teacher

1 Victoria Drummond was the daughter of Captain Malcolm Drummond, who was a groom-in-waiting to Queen Victoria. The queen was her godmother.

2 She was recognised as a qualified sea-going Second Engineer in 1924.

3 In 1926 she became the first woman in the world to hold a Chief Engineer's ticket.

4 Victoria took part in the Dunkirk evacuation in 1940, and the action described in the story above took place in mid-Atlantic when her ship was attacked by a German Condor plane.

5 She was the first woman ever to be awarded the Lloyd's War Medal for bravery at sea. The September link is with the beginning of World War Two in September, 1939.

Hymn suggestion

Come and Praise Vol 2 'O let us spread the pollen of peace' No 145

Prayer

Let us appreciate the talents which have been given to us. Let us have the wisdom to see opportunities to use these talents. Let us have the sensitivity to use them always for the good of others.

National Curriculum cross-curricular reference

This material could be linked to CDT, particularly with some practical problems which require the children to apply knowledge and skills in solving them. The importance of collaboration in problem-solving could be emphasised here too.

11 For good and evil . . .

Introduction

Close your mouths tightly. Now run your tongue round your teeth inside your mouth. Press it against the front teeth. Lick your lips with it. Now listen to this morning's story which is about . . .

Story

Long ago people in the West Indies believed that there was a god called Orula, who ruled the earth. How he got this job was one of their favourite stories.

The chief of all the gods decided that he would test the young god Orula to see if he was suitable for this difficult task.

He summoned Orula to him and said, 'Prepare me the best meal you can possibly think of.'

Orula bowed low and then went to do this. Some time later he came back with a large plate and set it down before the chief of the gods.

Round the outside of the plate were small pieces of salad, nuts and vegetables. In the centre of it was a large slice of beef tongue. The chief eyed it hungrily and then ate it all.

When he had finished he looked at Orula and nodded. 'That was splendid. I enjoyed it very much indeed. Tell me, why did you choose tongue?'

'Well,' replied Orula, 'it was really to show you how much good the tongue does on earth. It comforts people when they are worried, encourages them when they need help, explains their difficulties, speaks words of love and kindness – and can even tell jokes!'

'Hmm,' muttered the chief, stroking his chin, 'a good answer . . . yes, a good answer.'

There was a pause and then he spoke again.

'Now – bring me the worst meal you can think of.'

Once again Orula disappeared, to return shortly with another large plate. Lying on it was a thick slice of . . . beef tongue. With raised eyebrows the chief bit into a slice. Immediately his face creased and he spat it out.

'Ugh! That is disgusting, absolutely disgusting. Whatever made you choose tongue again?'

'Ah,' said Orula. 'We have heard how the tongue is an instrument for good – but it can also lie, spread false rumours, say hurtful things, cause trouble.'

The chief held up his hand. 'You're right of course – and such wisdom makes you the ideal person to rule the earth and deal with all its problems.'

And so Orula became god of the earth.

Information for the teacher

1 A possible follow-up could be to discuss some useful sayings, proverbs, etc. To make a September link, one of the most famous men of words was Dr Johnson. He was born on 18th September, 1709. Examples of his sayings:

'When two Englishmen meet their first talk is of the weather.'

'When a man is tired of London he is tired of life.'

2 Some useful quotations from religious and other sources could include:

If a man speaks or acts
With an evil thought,
Pain follows him.

A tamed mind
Brings happiness.   (Buddha)

Whoever loves life and would see good days
Must restrain his tongue from evil
And his lips from deceit;
Must turn from wrong and do good,
Seek peace and preserve it.   (The Bible, Peter 3, 8–11)

O God
Let us be united
Let us speak in harmony.   (Hindu prayer)

A word is like water,
Once spilled it cannot be gathered again.   (African proverb)

Hymn suggestion

Come and Praise Vol 1 'Go tell it on the mountain' No 24

Prayer

One of the passages from Teacher Information could be used here.

National Curriculum cross-curricular reference

Science, in terms of the tongue, speaking, hearing, could be followed up here. Locating the West Indies and learning something of the Caribbean could be a geographical link. Research into more proverbs, and making up some can extend the English work.

12 Jane

Introduction

People who are handicapped need all the help they can get. Blind people, for instance, are tremendously grateful for the wonderful work which is done by their guide dogs.

This morning's story is about Jane, a golden retriever guide dog. Jane not only looked after her mistress well, but also found time to help a person who could see!

Story

'Right Jane, I know we're coming to the road.'

Miss Lorann spoke to Jane, her guide dog, as if she were a human being, she relied on her so much.

Miss Lorann could hear but not see the busy traffic moving along the street of the town. Jane could both hear and see it, and she knew how dangerous it was.

When they reached the point where Miss Lorann usually crossed the road, Jane sat obediently on the kerb waiting for her mistress's signal saying that she was ready to cross.

Suddenly Miss Lorann heard a shout and then, with a terrible shock, she felt Jane's harness torn from her hand. There followed a whole series of noises which were quite terrifying for the blind woman. A car's tyres screeched in protest to an emergency stop, a child screamed and then began to cry, footsteps pounded around her and voices shouted nearby.

Miss Lorann was near to panic when she suddenly felt Jane's warm body press reassuringly against her legs.

'Oh Jane, thank goodness you're safe. What has happened?'

A man's voice spoke over the child's sobbing. 'That's a wonderful dog you've got there. She just saved a little girl's life.'

'But how . . .' began Miss Lorann, when a young woman's voice interrupted her and she felt herself being hugged.

'How can I ever thank you and your dog enough?' she gasped. 'Becky – that's my little girl – ran away from me and was just about to dash into the road when your dog saw her. The dog jumped in front of her and knocked her out of the way of the car you heard skidding.'

Miss Lorann smiled and held onto the young woman tightly for a few seconds. 'I'm so pleased Jane was able to help,' she said, 'but I'm not surprised. Jane is really a wonderful friend.'

Jane's story appeared in the newspapers and she was awarded a medal for her quick thinking and swift action.

Information for the teacher

1 The address for Guide Dogs for the Blind Association is: Alexandra House, 9–11 Park Street, Windsor, Berks SL4 1JR.
2 70 per cent of guide dogs are labradors and 70 per cent are bitches. The training period lasts from six to eight months.
3 The September link is that the first training of dogs for use with blind people began in Germany in 1916.

4 The 'animal VC' is the Dickin Medal, instituted by Mrs Maria Dickin in 1943.

Hymn suggestion

Come and Praise Vol 1 'Cross over the road' No 70

Prayer

Let us think this morning of those who are handicapped in some way. Let us pray that they may be given hope and help. Amen.

National Curriculum cross-curricular reference

An obvious link for this material is Science – 'health', 'handicaps', 'sight', 'animals' – all strands in this theme which can be examined in more detail.

13 The Victoria Cross

Introduction

There are many different kinds of courage. The Victoria Cross is the highest medal this country awards for courage in wartime. This is the story of how one young man won it.

Story

It was 15th September, 1940 and a Hampden bomber of the Royal Air Force was flying on a mission over Belgium in the early part of the Second World War. The pilot of the bomber was Flying Officer Connor and the wireless operator was Sergeant John Hannah.

'We are nearing the target.' The pilot alerted his crew over the intercommunication system.

'Keep a look out for . . .'

Flying Officer Connor couldn't finish the sentence because there was a terrific explosion in the plane. It had been hit by a shell. With engines screaming and flames already licking through the fuselage, the bomber dived earthwards as the pilot fought to regain control.

Finally Flying Officer Connor managed to get the plane levelled out but he knew they were in serious danger.

'Pilot to crew, pilot to crew,' he called over the intercom. 'I don't think I can get her back – bale out, bale out!'

The navigator and the rear gunner immediately put on their parachutes and jumped out of the plane. Sergeant John Hannah, however, looked at the raging flames and thought: 'If I bale out, the pilot will never get out in time. He'll be killed . . . but if I try to put the fire out . . .'

'Sir,' John's voice sounded in Flying Officer Connor's ears.

'What are you doing still on board? I told you to bale out,' replied the anxious pilot.

'I'm going to have a try at putting the fire out,' said John quietly.

Connor didn't say anything, but turning his head to look round he was horrified. Behind him was a wall of flames and the heat beat on his face.

Meanwhile John had started work with the fire extinguishers. There were great holes in the sides and floor of the plane and rounds of ammunition for the guns which lay on the floor kept exploding in the flames and flying in all directions. The metal doors in the plane had buckled and melted and the electrical equipment was on fire.

Refusing to be discouraged by the terrifying scene, John kept using one extinguisher after another to fight the flames, despite being almost suffocated by smoke and fumes. As he did so the plane juddered and sank lower and lower in the sky as it struggled homewards.

Finally, with the airfield in sight Flying Officer Connor felt a hand on his shoulder. 'Fire's out, sir,' said John in his quiet way.

Connor couldn't believe what his young, 18-year-old wireless operator had achieved, but he hadn't time to comment – the landing strip was coming up ahead.

Minutes later the cruelly damaged bomber landed. John jumped to the ground as if returning from a routine mission.

The next day, however, the plane was examined by experts. They could hardly believe what they saw. It seemed impossible that any aircraft could reach home after such damage had been suffered.

That it had done so, and the life of Flying Officer Connor had been saved, was due entirely to the courage of the young wireless operator. Sergeant John Hannah was awarded the Victoria Cross for his bravery.

Information for the teacher

1 The Victoria Cross was instituted in 1856. The medals used to be made from the metal of guns captured in the Crimea.
2 The Hampden bomber in this story was attacking German barges moored at Antwerp.
3 This assembly/story might be linked with a visit to somewhere like the Imperial War Museum, Lambeth Road, London SE1 6HZ, or its counterpart at RAF Duxford. For a list of museums and associations specifically to do with aeroplanes, a useful address is: The British Aircraft Preservation Council, 9 Brackley Road, Heaton Chapel, Stockport.

Hymn suggestion

Come and Praise Vol 1 'When a knight won his spurs' No 50

Prayer

Let us think this morning about some words from the Bible. Listen to them carefully: 'Prepare yourself for testing. Set a straight course, be resolute. Do not lose your head in time of disaster' (Ecclesiasticus 2, 1–2).

National Curriculum cross-curricular reference

There is a lot of scope here (and a great deal of material available) to link this story with work on a 'How we used to live' historical theme. Personal contacts with people like the children's grandparents is useful. Science, through Health and Safety, in the context of a 'fire' theme could be followed up.

14 Open wide

Introduction

We are lucky that most dental diseases can now be prevented if we look after our teeth and go to the dentist for regular check-ups. This is essential for our good health. When we go, everything about the dentist's surgery is spotlessly clean, the dentist usually wears a special blue or white coat and she or he makes sure the treatment is as painless as possible.

If you'd lived two or three hundred years ago, however, things would have been very different . . .

Story

'It's driving me mad,' said Josh. 'I can't eat, I can't sleep – I can hardly talk!'

'I know how you feel,' replied his friend Walter. 'There's nothing worse than toothache, but you'll be able to get help tomorrow, the dentist is coming to market day.'

'The dentist? Do you know anything about him? Is he good? Will it hurt?'

'Er . . . it's quite a nice day, isn't it?'

The next day the two friends were up early. Soon they were making their way with the jostling crowds towards the town. It was market day and the air was full of the shouts of buyers and sellers on their way to the town square.

Josh felt terrible. One side of his face was swollen and his bad tooth felt as if it were on fire. What made it worse was that every time he mentioned the dentist Walter changed the subject.

When they reached the market square the two men looked along the row of stalls and then noticed the small tent at the end of one of the rows.

'He's here,' said Walter, pointing towards it.

Outside the tent a heavy wooden chair stood unevenly on the rough ground. Beside it stood a large fat man in a rather dirty tunic. He was talking to two other rough-looking men and a smaller one, who had a large drum dangling from his neck. A great gust of coarse laughter interrupted their conversation and Josh had a strange feeling that they were just waiting for him.

'Come on,' said Walter. 'Let's get it over with. I'll tell them about the pain you're in.'

'It doesn't seem so bad now,' muttered Josh weakly.

A couple of minutes later he was sitting in the heavy wooden chair. The drummer stood to one side and the two rough-looking men lounged behind the chair.

The dentist pushed a large, dirty finger into Josh's mouth.

'At the back, isn't it? We'll soon have that beauty out!'

So saying he disappeared into the tent. What happened next Josh never forgot. The fat man re-emerged with a huge pair of pliers; at the same time the drummer started to thump the drum as loudly as he could; the two men behind the chair grabbed Josh's shoulders and held him down. The dentist approached . . .

Information for the teacher

1 This seems like a good point at which to stop the story. There are plenty of talking points to take from here – the lack of hygiene, proper care etc. then compared with now.
2 The drummer in this ritual was used to drown out the screams of the victim.
3 A point of reference for this story is that on 30th September 1846, an American dentist, Dr William Morton, performed the first extraction to be done whilst the patient was under an anaesthetic.
4 There is plenty of scope to follow this up with discussions of modern dental care and health education in terms of prevention.

Hymn suggestion

Come and Praise Vol 1 'Come my brother, praise the Lord' No 20

Prayer

Dear God, Let us give thanks for those who look after our health. Let us give thanks particularly this morning for the skill of dentists, and of those whose knowledge has helped treatment to become more effective and free of pain. Amen.

National Curriculum cross-curricular reference

There are considerable opportunities for linking this work with Science, Health Care – 'ourselves and healthy living'.

History can also be incorporated and the theme is one which also lends itself to graphic writing and description in English activities.

15 At the fair

Introduction

If somebody said to you, 'Let's go to the Fair', you would be pleased and probably excited. You would think of flashing lights, music, rides on roundabouts and dodgems, funny or interesting sideshows. But fairs weren't always like this.

Story

Matt kept bending the fingers of his left hand. When he did this the pain in his arm eased a bit and he could almost bend it properly.

'Well, I wonder who is going to pick us this time?' said Josiah, who stood next to Matt, shuffling in the cool autumn air.

Along with Matt and Josiah stood rows and rows of other men. They had all come to the Mop Fair on Michaelmas Day to offer themselves for hire for the coming year.

'I hope somebody does,' muttered Matt, as much to himself as Josiah.

He knew that the farmers picked only the strongest looking men to work on their farms for the year. And if you didn't get picked you didn't have any work . . . so you didn't eat and neither did your family.

Matt pulled his shoulders back and tried to look fit and keen to work. A ruddy-faced farmer stopped in front of him and Josiah: 'You two,' he said, 'done plenty of farm work?'

Josiah nodded. 'We certainly have. You won't find two better workers than us, boss.'

'Hmm, I wonder,' answered the farmer. Then shooting out his hand he grasped the muscles in Matt's left arm. Pain shot through Matt's arm like a stab of quick burning fire. Somehow he managed not to flinch.

'We can do anything those young'uns can do,' he managed to blurt out through gritted teeth.

Without a job he couldn't feed Martha and the children, and that didn't bear thinking about.

'Right,' said the farmer, making up his mind. 'Start tomorrow. You know the wages.'

Matt felt relief surge through him. He had a job for another year. Then the worry started again. How much longer would his arm last out? Could he stand the pain? Would anybody find out about it?

Information for the teacher

1 On the day after Michaelmas (29th September), every year after 1351 and the Statute of Labourers, agricultural labourers paraded with their implements at market towns all over the country. Each hoped to be hired for the coming year. After the hiring procedures a 'Mop Fair' was held.

2 Obviously Michaelmas (St Michael's Day) was a very important occasion in earlier years too. St Michael was often portrayed as a warrior with a spear, who killed Lucifer the rebel angel.

3 The eating of goose was a tradition on Michaelmas Day. One reason for furthering this was due to the fact that Queen Elizabeth I was eating goose when news of the great victory over the Spanish Armada was brought to her. She was so pleased that she said from that point on she would always eat goose on that particular day.

Hymn suggestion

Come and Praise Vol 2 'Michaelmas Daisies' No 137

Prayer

Dear God, Help us to appreciate how fortunate we are to live in this present day, when there are fewer hardships than in days gone by.

Please help those less fortunate people in other parts of the world for whom hardship, lack of work, education and food still make life very difficult. Amen.

National Curriculum cross-curricular reference

A quite substantial History theme could be built up round a Michaelmas anniversary – agriculture then and now; the Statute of Labourers; traditions/sayings/folklore associated with the time.

Work and Health can be considered in Science, and the technological advances of agricultural tools and machinery considered in CDT – in simple, practical terms in some cases.

October

16 On the roads

Introduction

Every day people are killed or injured on our roads. We must, at all times, be careful in traffic. Sometimes, however, when an accident does occur it is someone's bravery which saves lives.

Story

On an October day in a Hornsey courtroom a group of people were being praised for their courage.

'Without your bravery this man would have died,' said the coroner, Dr Vanezis.

He was talking about the road accident, from which Mr Shane Fowler was saved. Mr Fowler was in a Renault 21 car which crashed at a road junction in Enfield and burst into flames.

Keith Dear and his wife were out walking at the time. The terrible noise of the skid and the crunching of metal were followed by the whoosh of flame as the car caught fire.

'Come on,' shouted Mr Dear to his wife, 'we've got to get the driver out of there.'

The two of them ran towards the burning car. At the same time other pedestrians were racing to help too. All of them ignored the fact that the car, which was now lying on its side, could explode at any minute.

'Let's get it upright,' someone shouted.

'It's the only way we'll get him out.'

'Come on, all together – heave!'

Despite the pain of burnt hands and the choking smoke the group got the car back on its wheels.

'He's strapped in,' shouted Mr Dear.

'That's all right,' cried another voice, 'I've got a pocket knife. Let me through and I'll cut the seat belt straps.'

Moving forward as he spoke, the man with the knife began to saw frantically at the unconscious driver's seat belt. After what seemed an age the belt parted and the group found another difficulty – the car door was jammed and wouldn't open.

'We'll have to drag him through this open window,' said Mr Dear. As gently as they could, the rescuers eased the injured man from his car. Because he was unconscious and couldn't help, he was a dead weight and it was very difficult to get him through such a small space.

Whilst this struggle was going on the sound of an ambulance could be heard in the distance. Another pedestrian had rushed to call this.

By now Mr Fowler lay on the pavement.

'Come on, we can't let him stay here – this thing could go up any minute,' shouted Mr Dear. It was the first time anybody had mentioned the danger of an explosion.

As tenderly as possible, Mr Fowler was carried away from the scene of the crash. Soon the ambulance and the fire brigade arrived and experts took over. The rescuers quietly went home.

Later, when they had all been gathered together to hear Dr Vanezis's congratulations, they heard about how badly injured Mr Fowler had been.

With eight broken ribs, severe bruising and shock, he had had to stay in hospital for four weeks. Without the courage and quick action of Mr Dear and the others Mr Fowler would certainly have died.

Information for the teacher

1 Newspapers are a virtually inexhaustible source of stories like this. This one takes a positive approach, but sometimes a negative approach detailing the carelessness or irresponsibility of some road user is equally useful in getting a road safety message across to the children.
2 'Selflessness' is a useful theme into which this story would fit; there are many examples of people risking their lives for others. These could vary from those for whom it is a regular task – firemen, lifeboat crew members, industrial rescue workers, etc. to casual bystanders who act with courage and foresight as this group of people did.
3 An obvious Biblical link here is with the Good Samaritan (Luke 10).
4 A useful address in connection with this theme: The Royal Society

for the Prevention of Accidents, Cannon House, The Priory, Queensway, Birmingham B4 6BS.

Hymn suggestion

Come and Praise Vol 2 'I was lying in the roadway' No 88

Prayer

Dear God, Please give us the wisdom and care to use our roads well so that we don't endanger ourselves or others. Help us to remember the rules of the road so that we might do this.

Let us also give thanks for all those people who help so bravely when accidents do take place. Amen.

National Curriculum cross-curricular reference

Any work on road safety can include a great deal of Science and Maths (wheels, motion, maintenance, stopping distances, impacts, etc.). The link with the Good Samaritan could extend from Religious Education to English and Drama. The children can write, act and mime both traditional and modern versions of the story.

17   A tale of two sisters

Introduction

Lots of stories follow a similar pattern. There are good and bad people in them and at first it seems as if everything is going best for the bad person. Then there is a surprise twist which results in a happy ending.

Story

The sun shone down brightly on grass glistening after the shower. Floella pushed her way along the path towards the pool. It was very hot, as usual.

As she walked, Floella thought about her sister Jayna.

'Go and get some water from the pool, Floella,' Jayna had said, 'and hurry up about it.'

She never seemed to say anything gently or politely, thought Floella. And yet she was so beautiful, easily the loveliest girl in the village.

'Well nobody would ever say I was beautiful,' thought Floella as she glimpsed her reflection in a large puddle of water on the ground. A large, round, rather heavy face looked back at her.

Parting the last clump of bushes, Floella arrived at the pool and got a surprise. There, sitting by the water, was an incredibly old woman. Feebly she was trying to wash her back.

Seeing the old woman's difficulties Floella called out to her. 'It's all right – let me help you. I can wash your back for you quite easily.'

The old woman's back was hard and scaly and Floella had to wash very hard to soften and clean it. At last she finished.

'You're so kind,' said the old woman in a surprisingly gentle voice. 'How nice of you to give so much of your time to a miserable old woman.'

'Oh, don't say that,' replied Floella, 'it wasn't anything; I'm just glad I was able to help.'

'Well,' went on the old woman, 'I'd like to reward you for your kindness, my dear. You can have any wish you like.'

'Oh, I couldn't possibly take anything,' replied Floella. 'I'm just glad that we've met and had a chance to talk.'

The old woman smiled.

'Look in the water my dear.'

Floella did so – and gasped. The face that looked back at her was still her own, but different. The round, heavy look had gone and, there was no doubt about it, she was beautiful.

'Oh . . . but . . . thank . . .'

She looked up, but the old woman had vanished.

When Floella got home Jayna didn't recognise her at first, but after listening to only part of the story she snapped in her usual unkind way. 'Trust you to have all the luck. I suppose you think you are more beautiful than me now. Well you're not and nobody else will think so either.'

But even while she was talking Jayna was thinking how she could get something for herself. As soon as Floella was out of the way she hurried to the pool.

'What did that sister of mine say?' she muttered to herself as she hurried along the path. 'There was somebody who told her she could have anything she liked. Wait till I find this person, I'm going to ask to be the richest girl in the world.'

Impatiently she burst through the bushes surrounding the pool – and saw an old, feeble woman by the water.

'Could you . . . could you help me wash my back please?' asked the old woman in a thin, wavering voice.

'This creature can't be granting wishes,' thought Jayna contemptuously, and snapped angrily at the old woman.

'Get out of my way. I'm looking for somebody important. Come on – move!'

A tired smile flickered across the old woman's face. 'As you are so rude and impatient perhaps you'd better look like me,' she said.

At once Jayna changed from a beautiful girl into a gnarled and tired looking old woman.

Information for the teacher

1 This story is an adaptation of a West Indian folk tale and is similar to many such stories which can be found in children's anthologies. Teachers might find the Biblical tale of the unforgiving servant a useful link. It can be found in Matthew 18, 23–34.

2 An October link for this story is that various towns in England hold Festivals of literature at this time of the year, and these provide an excellent opportunity to look at the messages of stories.

Hymn suggestion

Come and Praise Vol 1 'God knows me' No 15

Prayer

Dear God, Let us think this morning about some words, and what they mean – kindness, helpfulness, selfishness, greed, forgiveness.

Give us the strength to be kind and thoughtful to everyone with whom we come in contact. Help us always to be considerate people. Amen.

National Curriculum cross-curricular reference

Obviously, with its literary links, this theme would provide a great deal of English work. Similar stories could be found to contrast and compare and much dramatic work could ensue.

Both History and Geography can be interwoven with folk tales, their time and source.

18 Mums

Introduction

This morning's assembly is about mums. Listen to what some children have written.

Mums

1 One of my best times in the week is on a Wednesday night when I go swimming with my mum. We have a cup of tea really early and then later we drive down to Waltham Abbey and go to the pool.

My mum is a real good swimmer and she always dives in. I'm a bit scared and sometimes I jump in. Then we swim together up and down the pool doing breaststroke and backstroke. We have a lot of fun in the changing room and we have a hot shower.

Then we run to the car and on our way home we stop and buy fish and chips. When we get home dad is back from work and he is pleased to see us – and the fish and chips!

2 One of the worst times I have ever had was when mum was in hospital for a week. Every night we went to see her and she was in her dressing gown and I wanted her to come home with us. I thought she looked sad when we left even though she was smiling.

My dad is not a very good cook and we have had burnt stuff to eat. And he didn't make the bed properly because I looked in their room. I didn't like seeing all mum's stuff, her lipstick and things, when she wasn't there.

When mum came home it was good, and I hope she doesn't go to hospital again.

3 I want to tell you about my mum. She's quite big really and has blonde hair. She wears jeans in the house but dresses when she goes out. Her favourite food is lasagne and she likes mints. She sometimes wears high heeled shoes but she says they kill her feet. She's got quite a soft voice but when she laughs it's loud. She laughs a lot because she likes jokes.

My mum has got lovely hands and I love to feel them on my face.

Information for the teacher

1 This material could obviously be supplemented or replaced by passages written by children known to the teacher.
2 An October link for this material is with the Hindu festival of Durga (which takes place in the month of *Asvin*). The goddess Durga, 'the divine mother' in one of her forms, is particularly remembered on Durga Puja (1st Asvin), when daughters return to their mother's homes for feasting, celebrations and the giving of presents.

Hymn suggestion

Come and Praise Vol 2 'Love will never come to an end' No 99

Prayer

Dear God, Help us to think for a moment about mothers all over the world. Let us give thanks for their love by saying the following prayer together. (*The children could repeat the words one line at a time after the teacher*):

> Where love is
> There riches be.
> Keep us all
> From poverty (Old Medieval Prayer)

National Curriculum cross-curricular reference

English, in several forms, is possibly the most productive National Curriculum subject with regard to this theme. The subject is one children feel confident with and their own work can be supplemented by some useful literary references. Some of Michael Rosen's poems are valuable here because they often focus on family life. In direct contrast to the witty and amusing Rosen, the last page of that famous and moving book *I am David* by Anne Holm (Puffin) provides sensitive and evocative reading.

Art is also another obvious link here.

19 What is it called?

Introduction

We give and use names for all sorts of things. For a start, we all have names by which we are known. Then there are names we would like to be called – and others which we would not like being called. Let's think a little bit more about names . . .

Story

If your birthday is in October then you were born under a particular star sign. For instance, if you were born between 1st and 22nd of the month you were born under Libra – and are thoughtful and have a strong sense of fair play. If you were born after the 22nd October, you enjoy your own company and don't like to be bothered by other people and your star sign is Scorpio.

If you were born in the British Isles in a British family your Christian name comes first, followed by your surname – for example, John Brown. For people born in China, however, the surname comes first. Sikh children have other names too: boys are called *Singh* which means *lion* and girls are called *Kaur* which means *princess*.

Names are often shortened or changed: William – Bill; Margaret – Maggie; Jacqueline – Jackie; Robert – Bob and so on. Usually people enjoy their shortened name which is special to them, but people don't always enjoy nicknames which are given to them. Sometimes such names are cruel and unkind and make the person called in this way very unhappy.

There are other names which we all like to be called – friend, hero, star, honest, reliable, kind; and just as many we would not like to be called – enemy, coward, fool, liar, unreliable, mean.

Other names make us think of nice things – rose, holiday, Christmas. Then again there are those which cause unpleasant thoughts – pain, filth, loneliness.

With so many names in the world our last thoughts might be helped by William Shakespeare. He said that if we are robbed of our 'good name' we become 'poor indeed'. What do you think this means?

Information for the teacher

1 The actual quotation to which the last paragraph refers is:

> He that filches from me my good name
> Robs me of that which enriches him not
> And makes me poor indeed.

2 Making a list of significant and thought-provoking names associated with October could be a useful exercise. Harvest and Hallowe'en are possible starters here.

3 Genesis 2, 19 contains some Biblical comment on naming.

4 A great deal of follow-up work may be done on religious names – Bible, Qur'an, Cross, Church, Temple, Vicar, Rabbi, Imam, etc.

Hymn suggestion

Come and Praise Vol 1 'At the name of Jesus' No 58

Prayer

Let us remember that a good name is earned by the way we behave towards others.

Let us remember that a good name is hard to earn but easy to lose.

Let us remember that we are judged by what we say and what we do.

National Curriculum cross-curricular reference

Geography could feature in a simple study of names in different languages, messages of greeting and farewell. Both creative and factual writing about names would encompass English work.

20 Saved by a horse

Introduction

Sometimes on special occasions in London, horses can be seen pulling along carriages. Some of the most famous of these are the magnificent Whitbread shire horses. This is a story about one of them.

Story

'Come on there my beauties – giddup!'

Charlie Gardener had driven drays pulled by Whitbread shire horses for many years. On a brisk October morning in 1953 things were a little different because he had a new horse partnering his old friend Gracie.

'Come on Gracie – show him how it's done,' chuckled Charlie.

Between the shafts of the dray Gracie felt her master's tug on the reins and knew he would look after them in the busy London traffic.

For a time all went well, and then Gracie felt the reins go slack – and Charlie's encouragement and instruction could no longer be heard.

The horses of course had no idea that Charlie had collapsed unconscious in his seat. Seriously ill as he was, the reins dangled loosely in his hands and the horses and their mighty wagon were out of control in the hectic traffic.

Gracie, however, sensed that something was wrong – and she wasn't one of the famous Whitbread shire horses for nothing! Keeping a steady pace and making her companion follow suit, she clattered through the streets to the destination she knew best – the stables in Garrett Street.

Eventually Gracie turned into the narrow side street out of the main hustle and bustle. Then, as soon as she had stopped, she began to neigh, stamp her feet and throw her head about. Hearing this most unusual behaviour the stablemen rushed out – and saw Charlie slumped, apparently lifeless, in his seat.

Quickly they lifted the sick man down and he was rushed to hospital. Thankfully he made a full recovery and when he returned to Garrett Street it was with many an extra lump of sugar for Gracie.

'There can't be too many men who can say their life was saved by a horse,' he chuckled, patting Gracie's head.

Information for the teacher

1 Whitbread's shire horses have been pulling drays through the streets of London for over two hundred years. There are still stables in Garrett Street.

2 There are plenty of Biblical references to horses. When the Persians wanted to honour a man he was royally dressed and led through the streets on horseback (Esther 6, 9–11). Horses in Biblical times wore no shoes, were driven with bit and bridle and

they often wore bells. The horses of rich men were decorated with handwoven material.

Hymn suggestion

Come and Praise Vol 1 'All creatures of our God and King' No 7

Prayer

Dear God, Help us in our responsibilities towards animals. Teach us to care for them properly and make us aware of their needs. Help us to value the pleasure, and often help, which they give us. Amen.

National Curriculum cross-curricular reference

The link with History is obvious and can be pursued in themes such as famous horses; horses who have helped men, etc. Horses in children's literature are quite common – Black Beauty, the Red Pony, etc. – and this could be followed up in English.

Science could be involved in an appropriate study of horses – size, weight, skeleton, characteristics, speed, uses, etc.

As children (and adults!) find horses very difficult to draw, work in Art could involve making pictorial horses from cut-out materials, tissue paper, papier mâché, etc.

21 Learning a lesson

Introduction

Long ago, in the days before banks, people who saved money had plenty of worries about keeping it safe. Should they hide it? If so where? Or could they give it to someone powerful to look after it for them? Listen to what happened to one unfortunate man.

Story

'You see, sir,' said the poor man, 'I have saved one hundred crowns but need another fifty before I can go back to my wife and children and buy a small piece of land.'

'Go on,' said the rich merchant.

'Well I know you have many servants to look after your property and I have heard you are an honest man. Will you look after my hundred crowns until I can save the rest and return to my family? I will pay for your help.'

'Pay?' smiled the merchant. 'Don't worry about that – I'm a man who likes to help when he can. Your money will be safe with me.'

'Thank you,' replied Abraham, for that was the poor man's name.

Back to the fields he went to work long and tiring days. He hadn't seen his family for three years . . . but soon, he could return and care for them. The months passed and finally Abraham had the rest of his money. He then went to see the merchant.

'A hundred crowns! What are you talking about? I've never seen you before in my life. Servants – throw this scoundrel out!'

Abraham couldn't believe his ears when he heard the merchant's angry roaring. Within minutes he was lying bruised and bleeding in the street, where he had been thrown by the servants. His precious hundred crowns! Gone! Nobody would ever believe his side of the story . . . three years' work for nothing. Abraham clasped his hands over his face in despair.

'What's the matter old chap? It can't be as bad as all that.' A kind voice interrupted Abraham's thoughts and a friendly arm held his shoulder. Looking up, Abraham saw a man with sharp, intelligent eyes who was well spoken and well dressed. Desperate with disappointment and frustration Abraham told the stranger the whole story.

'Hmm, seems like our friend needs a lesson,' said the stranger. 'This is what we'll do.'

The next day the well spoken stranger stood in front of the merchant.

'I've heard you are a man to be trusted,' he said. 'I too am a merchant making a journey to lands of the east. However, I am worried about carrying my fortune with me. Would you look after half of it for me until I get back?'

The merchant's eyes glinted greedily. Quickly he smiled and replied in a fawning voice.

'Oh you can certainly trust me, sir. Shall we get on with making the arrangements about . . .'

Before he could go on there was an interruption and a servant showed Abraham into the room.

'Oh no,' thought the treacherous merchant. 'What a time for him to appear again.' But before he could speak he got a surprise.

'Sir,' said Abraham politely, as if nothing had happened on his previous visit. 'I've come to collect my hundred crowns.'

The merchant did some quick thinking. He needed to impress the stranger who was obviously going to leave a far greater sum of money so . . .

'Of course, my friend,' he said, pretending too that nothing had happened between them. 'At once, at once.'

Within minutes Abraham had his hundred coins and hurried out.

'There you are – you see how reliable I am,' said the merchant, turning to his rich visitor, but in the commotion with Abraham the mysterious stranger had slipped away.

Later that night, as Abraham and the stranger journeyed far from the town the two men smiled at each other.

'Thanks,' said Abraham, 'somebody learned a lesson in honesty today.'

Information for the teacher

1 A possible October reference here is to Al Capone. The American gangster who thought he could live beyond the law was sent to prison for income tax evasion on 17th October, 1931.

Hymn suggestion

Come and Praise Vol 2 'A still, small voice' No 96

Prayer

Let us think this morning of the 'still, small voice' of our conscience. Let us ask that we might learn the lessons of honesty. Let us behave towards others as we would like them to behave to us.

Let us pray that our thoughts, words and deeds are guided towards these aims.

National Curriculum cross-curricular reference

There is great scope for links with English here. The story is ideal for drama and could provoke a great deal of discussion. The theme could be extended to encourage children to write individual stories of their own concerned with people 'learning their lessons'.

22   *One autumn afternoon*

Introduction

Sometimes, and unexpectedly, we meet wild creatures. Usually they dash away very quickly but in the passage which follows, a girl tells of her unusual meeting in a wood.

Story

My mum works at a field studies centre. This is a classroom in a beautiful wood. One day in the autumn half-term she let me go to work with her. While she was busy in her office I went for a walk in the wood.

It was late in the afternoon and the sun was shining through the trees in lovely shafts of light. I followed the path which went past the dining room and the camp fire bowl. There were squirrels everywhere and some of them were cheeky enough to come right up to my feet.

Without really thinking where I was going, my feet took me down the steep path to the brook. This wasn't flowing very quickly and when I looked up and around from its banks I could see a thin carpet of coloured leaves with, here and there, brightly patterned fungi poking upwards.

I must have been at the brook for about two minutes when I heard a rustling noise. The hairs on the back of my head seemed to stand on end and I felt as if I was a statue. What could it be?

Then, on the other side of the brook, a beautiful deer came into view. When it reached the water it bent its head to drink. I could see everything about it – its smooth brown coat and long legs; its small and pointed feet. Then, as I stood frozen to the spot, it lifted its head and looked straight at me. It didn't seem afraid or hurried.

For what seemed an age I stared at the deer and it stared back at me with huge brown eyes which seemed kind and gentle. Then suddenly, there was the cracking of twigs as the caretaker's dog chased some far-off rabbit. The deer turned, and raising its front legs in a twisting, bounding motion it moved away as quickly and smoothly as it had come.

I still stood there. The slanting sun's rays were fading now and the whole wood was growing dark quickly. I had a strange feeling of peace . . . almost as if I was special for a moment . . . and then . . .

'Elizabeth – where are you?'

It was my mother's voice. Suddenly I wanted to tell her my secret.

(by Elizabeth, aged 11)

Information for the teacher

1 The deer which Elizabeth saw in a Hertfordshire wood was a Muntjak.
2 Animal camouflage could be discussed here as it is one reason why so much wild life is not easy to see.
3 The rapport which can exist between man and animal is a subject which could be followed up in connection with this piece.

Hymn suggestion

Come and Praise Vol 1 'All things bright and beautiful' No 3

Prayer

Let us think this morning about all those creatures of field and wood for whom the coming of winter means a time of hardship. We pray that the autumn allows them to prepare for this time.

National Curriculum cross-curricular reference

Science and 'living creatures' is an obvious link here. This passage has a sensitivity which could also initiate writing in a similarly sensitive vein, particularly with children at the top end of the Junior School.

23 Honesty

Introduction

Unfortunately all of us are tempted to do something we shouldn't at some time or other. This morning's story is about a man who learned his lesson in a very unusual way.

Story

Johann and Karl made violins. Johann was getting old and relied more and more on his younger partner, Karl.

One day the old man put his arm round his young partner's shoulders. 'Karl,' he said, 'for years we've made the finest violins in the world. Great musicians have played them and thanked us for their quality.'

'That's true,' replied Karl, 'and we have played them ourselves in many concerts too.'

'Right,' went on Johann, 'but I'm getting old and tired my friend – and I want you to do me one last favour.'

'Anything,' said Karl.

'Well, the doctor says I must take a long holiday in the mountains. When I come back I would like a really great violin to play. Will you make me this great violin whilst I am away?'

'Of course I will,' answered Karl. 'It will be ready for you to come back to.'

'Remember,' continued Johann, 'use only the very finest materials; make it as only you know how.'

Soon the older man was away in the mountains. Karl sat alone in their workshop surrounded by the wood, strings and varnish. As he looked into the dancing flames of the open fire he thought deeply.

'I've got lots of work to do,' he thought. 'I haven't really got time to make this special violin for Johann . . . but . . . now he is so old, he'll never know if I use poorer materials and fake it up to look good. It will never last, of course, but he won't be around long enough to find out.'

So Karl got on with making other violins and when he had a spare moment he worked on Johann's, using just enough time and skill to make it look good, even though it wasn't.

'In five years' time this will just be scrap,' he thought, as he picked up another piece of poor wood and began to smooth it. He quickly put the thought out of his head.

Then came the day when Johann returned. Looking ill but rested, he came into the workshop.

'Johann, my old friend,' Karl greeted him warmly.

'Well,' said the old man, 'have you got it?'

Karl went to a cupboard and came back with the gleaming new violin. He held it out to Johann.

'Try it.'

'No, no,' said the old man. 'I know you will have used the best possible materials, and spared no time or expense on it. I will give you the money for all that.'

'Yes, but . . .'

'The violin is my present to you, Karl – in thanks for all our work together and all your help. I know you still play at many concerts and I want you to have a fine instrument which will sound beautiful and look good for years. Knowing you as I do I thought that this was the best way for you to get such an instrument.'

Information for the teacher

1 An October link for this honesty and dishonesty theme could be made on the 12th of the month – the date on which Elizabeth Fry, reformer of English prisons, died in 1845.
2 The theme of this particular story could be adapted to other products and situations quite easily. In any of its guises it is particularly well suited to drama.
3 There is a nice simple Biblical reference here: 'God loves people who tell the truth' (Proverbs 12, 22).

Hymn suggestion

Come and Praise Vol 2 'Make us worthy Lord' No 94

Prayer

> Do all the good you can,
> By all the means you can,
> In all the places you can,
> At all the times you can,
> To all the people you can,
> As long as ever you can. (John Wesley)

National Curriculum cross-curricular reference

Science and CDT are very relevant issues here in a 'construction' context – materials needed, care and planning needed, the rewards/ dangers of good/poor workmanship. There is plenty of scope for both practical activity and discussion.

English could feature in other, made-up versions of the story; these may be dramatised. Music could be involved in examining and listening to a violin.

24 *The rich and the poor*

Introduction

Look at this coin (*hold up a 50p coin*). October 14th is its birthday. In 1969 it first began to be used in Britain.

Money is very useful but lots of it does not necessarily bring happiness. This morning's story is about a rich man and a poor man, and what happens to them both.

Story

Abdul was a rich man and Ali was a poor one. They lived near each other and Abdul was very jealous of his neighbour. This was because Ali was cheerful and kind and people liked him. Abdul was mean and surly and people kept away from him.

'Why should Ali be so popular?' thought the mean Abdul. 'I'll fix him once and for all.'

Abdul went to the shop where Ali worked.

'That Ali – he's no good,' he said to the shopkeeper. 'You want to get rid of him.'

'Oh no, he's a good worker,' replied the shopkeeper. 'I . . .'

'Who is your best customer? Who supplies you with your finest cloth? Who owns the building this shop is in?'

When the shopkeeper heard Abdul asking these questions he knew he hadn't a chance. Abdul could ruin him. 'All right,' he said sadly. 'Ali goes tomorrow.'

So Ali lost his job, but he didn't know why he had lost it. A few days later he spent the last of his savings on a bowl of food for his family. He was taking this home when he slipped and bowl and food flew into the mud.

'Ah well,' thought Ali, 'something's bound to turn up.'

Cleaning the bowl, he stuck it on his head, and wandered down to the docks. Seeing some sailors loading a ship he stopped to help them.

'You're a good worker,' said one of the sailors. 'Why don't you come with us on this trip? One of the crew is sick. Pay's not bad.'

'Right,' said Ali.

He sent a message home and set sail. However, disaster struck when the ship was out at sea. A sudden storm blew up and a gigantic wave swept Ali overboard. After struggling in the sea for hours he was washed up on an island. Some natives helped him and he was taken before the chief.

'You had a lucky escape,' said the chief after listening to Ali's story, 'but tell me – why do you wear that thing on your head?'

Ali was puzzled – then he remembered he was still wearing the wooden food bowl stuck on his head.

'Oh,' he said, without really thinking, 'it's a special hat to keep your head cool.'

'Really?' remarked the chief. 'Well, it's always hot here on this island – can I try it?'

'Certainly, certainly,' said Ali kindly, and put the bowl on the chief's head. It was a perfect fit.

The chief walked round in the sun for about ten minutes.

'It's marvellous!' he said. 'Fantastic! It keeps your head really cool. I'd like to buy it from you.'

'No, no,' said Ali, 'have it as a gift. It will be my pleasure.'

The chief nodded gratefully. 'I couldn't take it for nothing. Please accept these in exchange.'

He snapped his fingers and a servant gave Ali a bag. It was full of precious stones, of which the island had thousands.

Soon after a boat was found to take Ali home. There he sold the precious stones for enough money to last him for the rest of his life. His family was delighted.

Abdul heard them celebrating.

'What could he have to celebrate?' he thought, and marched down the hill to find out.

Now Ali had no idea that it was Abdul who had caused him to lose his job. When he saw his neighbour, he called to him to come in. Over a glass of wine he told Abdul the whole story.

That night Abdul could hardly contain his excitement. If this stupid chief could give Ali a fortune for a wooden bowl, what might he give to somebody who brought him some real presents?

Next morning Abdul got to work. He sold off lots of his goods and bought some marvellous presents for the island chief. Then he hired a ship and crew and set sail. A few days later he stood before the chief.

'Your highness,' he said, 'people far and wide have heard of your great wisdom. As I was passing your island I felt it would be a privilege if I could offer you some humble gifts.'

At a signal, Abdul's men brought fabulous clothes, silks, satins, goblets, wonderful food – and laid them before the chief.

The chief was astounded.

Finally, after looking at all that lay before him, he spoke. 'Truly you are an amazingly generous man,' he said. 'I cannot accept these gifts without giving you something in return. You shall have our greatest treasure.'

Abdul, with head bowed, could hardly contain himself. 'This must be something really special,' he thought.

The chief clapped his hands and a large basket was brought to him. Lifting the lid the chief reached inside and with a kind smile handed over to Abdul Ali's wooden food bowl. (Adapted from an Egyptian folk tale.)

Information for the teacher

1 This is one of many stories which, by their use in assemblies, seek to indicate to children the way to better relationships between human beings. Such stories can be acted as well as they can be told.
2 Other good sources for similar material are tales of Anansi, Brer Rabbit and Nasr-ud-Din.
3 Useful Bible references about greed include: Mark 10, 17–30; Luke 12, 13–21; Mark 12, 41–44.

Suggested humn

Come and Praise Vol 1 'Think of a world without any flowers' No 17

Prayer

Let us pray this morning that we are neither greedy for more for ourselves nor envious of those who seem to have more than we do.

Let us remember that there is always someone worse off than we are.

Let us pray that those people in need may be given hope and encouragement. Amen.

National Curriculum cross-curricular reference

As this tale comes from Egypt, then a geographical location and comment on relevant issues – food, climate, etc. – would be appropriate.

'Values' could expand the Religious Education theme further and be used in a mathematical sense as well – the cost of feeding a family, etc.

25 *A father's choice*

Introduction

Have you ever wanted something really desperately? It might have been a computer, or a new bike, or a TV in your bedroom. Did you get it? If not, why not?

Story

Darren had just got his driving licence and he wanted a car. He had no money to buy one but he had an idea.

'Dad,' he said one morning to his father after breakfast. 'I want to talk to you for a few minutes.'

'Certainly, son, what is it?'

'Well, both Wayne and I work for you in the family business. That means that when you . . . er . . . when you . . .'

'Yes, yes, when I die. Come on, get to the point.'

'Well the business will be shared between us then, Dad, but I want to leave the firm and have my share of the money now.'

There was a long pause whilst Darren's father looked at him very seriously.

'Very well,' he said finally. 'I'll let you have your share tomorrow.'

So Darren got half of the money due to him from the family business. The next day he was at a new car showroom in the nearest town.

'I was thinking of getting something second hand,' he thought, 'but now I've got plenty of money I might as well get just what I want.'

Two days later Darren was behind the wheel of a shiny new red sports car. With two cases in the back he was leaving home for ever to find adventure. When he reached the big city he rented a flat in an expensive district. His car attracted a lot of interest and in no time he had a group of good friends.

'How fast can she go, Darren?'

'Why don't we take a trip to the coast?'

'Let's take your car, Darren, it's better than any of ours.'

Life was exciting. There always seemed to be something happening and Darren couldn't believe his popularity as he took his friends here, there and everywhere.

Then one day he realised that his money was beginning to run out.

'It'll be all right though,' he thought. 'I'll soon get a job and until I do my friends will see me OK.'

It was then that Darren got the first of a few unpleasant surprises. When he wasn't providing the transport his so-called friends lost interest in him. Desperate to keep their friendship, he set about finding a job to increase his rapidly falling money supply.

Times were hard though and he couldn't get the sort of job for which his father had trained him. He had to take a poorer job, with poorer wages. This meant moving to a rented room in a less attractive part of town. Now his lovely car had to stand out on a dark and dirty street.

Then came another dreadful day.

'Want to see you,' said the boss when Darren got to work. 'Afraid we're losing business so you'll have to go. Finish tonight.'

Depressed, Darren walked back through the rain to his room and there, outside on the street, stood his car – tyres slashed and paintwork scratched all over. As he now had no money he couldn't get it repaired and had to sell it as it was, for just a fraction of what he had paid for it.

A week later Darren sat in his cold, gloomy room. He hadn't been able to get another job, his last few pounds had gone to pay the rent and all he could afford for a meal was a cheap tin of meat which tasted suspiciously like cat food.

His mind turned to home. He thought of his old room, the lovely meals his mother made, the kindness of his father.

'I'll go back,' he said to himself, 'but I'll ask my father if I can be just an ordinary worker – I'm not fit to be called his son.'

A few days later Darren climbed down from the cab of the lorry which had given him a lift. He was tired, dirty and hungry because he had been hitchhiking for two days. He hadn't been able to afford the fare for either bus or train but now, standing outside the garden gate of his old house, he felt a great surge of relief sweep over him. It was then that his father, who happened to be looking out of the window, saw Darren. Dropping everything he rushed outside and hugged his son.

'You're back, you're back!' he cried. 'How wonderful. We'll have the best meal we've ever had in this house tonight!'

'But Dad,' mumbled Darren. 'I'm so ashamed. I've let you down, I've lost . . .'

'Come in, come in – let's get this party organised.'

And so the family was together again. At first, Darren's brother Wayne was not very happy about all the fuss being made over someone who had wasted his father's money. The boys' father took Wayne to one side.

'I know how you feel,' he said. 'But remember, everything I have is yours and it was certainly right for me to welcome Darren back. After all he was lost and now he's found again.'

Information for the teacher

1 A comparison between this modern version and the original story of the prodigal son can be made by referring to Luke 15. Some questions might be put to the children after reading the original – the son's thoughts when he was at his lowest ebb (verses 17–19); the father's joy at his son's return (verse 20); the father's comments (verse 24). St Luke's Day is 18th October.
2 This story could lead to some work on an enlarged theme of forgiveness. A useful quotation here might be:
   'Lord, how often am I to forgive my brother if he goes on worrying me? As many as seven times?'
   Jesus replied, 'I do not say seven times, I say seventy times seven.' (Matthew 18, 21–22)

Hymn suggestion

Come and Praise Vol 2 'Let the world rejoice together' No 148

Prayer

Dear God, Help us to know when we are wrong about something. Help us to say sorry and ask for forgiveness. Please help us also to forgive other people who may at times be thoughtless and unkind.
   Let us learn from your example. Amen.

National Curriculum cross-curricular reference

Whilst this is a very powerful Religious Education theme, there is a lot of scope for imaginative English work here also: discussion, creative and imaginative writing and drama.

26 *Confucius*

Introduction

Many people think that a certain Chinese man was the wisest person who ever lived. His name was Confucius and he was born over two thousand years ago.

Story

The music teacher looked up at the very tall, awkward young man.

'Very well, Confucius, if you want to learn the zither I will try to teach you.'

So Confucius began to learn to play the stringed instrument. But whatever the teacher told him to do the sound somehow didn't seem to come out right.

After listening to his pupil practise a piece for what seemed like the twentieth time the teacher lost his patience. 'Perhaps you're not cut out to play a musical instrument,' he said. 'You should try something else.'

'No, no,' replied Confucius. 'It doesn't sound right yet because I've got to master each aspect of the music.'

'What do you mean?' asked the teacher.

'Well first of all there is the tune itself, then there is the rhythm, then there is the atmosphere of the music, and the mood the man who wrote the music wanted me to feel.'

'But that terrible noise you're making,' went on the irritated teacher, 'how can that possibly help you to get all those things right?'

'Because I've got to be patient,' replied Confucius. 'All this practice sounds awful but I am gradually mastering all those things I mentioned.'

'Humph,' muttered the teacher and stamped off, leaving his pupil to it.

A few more days went by and the teacher happened to be passing the room where Confucius did his practising. From it came the most beautiful sounds. The teacher was astonished.

'It can't be . . .' he mumbled to himself.

Stepping through the doorway he saw Confucius's fingers stroking a wonderful melody from the zither.

'Now it all fits together,' smiled the wisest of men.

Information for the teacher

1 Confucius (Kung Fu Tzu) was born in Shandong (Shantung) to poor parents. He never achieved any high office and was self-taught. His philosophy has had a tremendous and long-lasting influence.
2 Physically Confucius was exceptionally tall, awkward and unprepossessing in appearance – another example of 'the worth lying within'.

3 The keynote of Confucius's teaching is *reciprocity*: behave to others as you would like them to behave to you.

Hymn suggestion

Come and Praise Vol 1 'The wise may bring their learning' No 64

Prayer

Our prayers this morning are based on the thoughts and words of Confucius. He said that we should use our eyes and ears to help us learn; we should use our face to show kindness and our manners to show respect. Our words should be true and our dealings with other people should always be fair.

National Curriculum cross-curricular reference

Geography could be involved in the location of Beijing (Peking) and Shandong (Shantung) and China. In the main, however, English would be best served by this subject, and a comparison made with Aesop's fables, proverbs, Biblical teachings, etc. These could provide food for discussion and debate.

27 *This month*

Introduction

> October is a piper, piping in the dell,
> Sad, sweet songs of sunshine,
> Summer's last farewell.

This month

Whilst October is very definitely the end of summer, it is still an interesting month for bird watchers. Many birds which are normally seen alone or in pairs now gather in much greater numbers. This, together with the fact that trees are losing their leaves, gives us a better chance to look at them – so watch out for flocks of magpies, long-tailed tits and greenfinches.

Apart from migrating birds, there are others coming from further north to spend the winter here. Field-fares and redwings are two examples. Remember too, leave a few apples on bird tables at this time of the year. They may stay there awhile but when water starts to freeze birds will be glad of them as a substitute drink.

Lots more squirrels can be seen about this month and with the feeling of the animal world stocking up for winter, you might like to think about some unusual graces which we could say before our meals. For instance:

> Heavenly Father bless us
> And keep us all alive;
> There's ten of us for dinner
> And not enough for five.

Look out for beautiful things this month too. Fruit, berries and leaves give the countryside some lovely colours. There may still be blackberries around but beware, don't pick them after 11th October! This is because of an old story which says that the devil was thrown out of Heaven and landed in a blackberry bush – and every year he remembers this on 11th October!

You might like to think about the weather this month too. It is often damp and misty, but people once believed that the weather in October foretold what was to come later. For instance:

> When berries are many in October
> Beware a hard winter.

> Rain in October
> Means wind in December.

It would be interesting to make observations on a weather chart this month to see if these things really do happen later in the winter.

Information for the teacher

1 This is also the time of the year when fungi can be sought and examined. Two easy-to-find favourites are pixie cups and fly agaric.
2 Apples are a source for much interesting work. There was once a custom that an apple tree should be planted whenever there was the birth of a son in a family. Simple cooking with children could involve apple muffins, baked apples, toffee apples.
3 The appreciation of the beauty of different coloured leaves could be enhanced in the classroom by leaf pictures, mobiles of leaves and wood, leaf prints.

Hymn suggestion

Come and Praise Vol 1 'Autumn Days' No 4

Prayer

Dear God, Help us to use our senses in this month of October so that we can see the beauty around us, hear the cries of the birds, smell the mists and dampness, taste the fruits of the season.

Thank you for all the pleasures of the natural world. Amen.

National Curriculum cross-curricular reference

The environmental studies aspect of Science is particularly well-catered for in this work. Similarly Art possibilities are wide-reaching and could involve the use of many natural materials, such as leaves, twigs, seeds, etc.

Music and Drama, both separately and together, are other links and a variety of music could be used in this context: Beethoven's 6th Symphony 'The Pastoral', Vivaldi's 'Four seasons', 'Persephone' – stories in movement.

28   A life's work

Introduction

Can you name some of the famous buildings in London? (*In answer to this question it should not be long before somebody says* St Paul's Cathedral.)

Story

A small, frail man stepped carefully amongst the charred timbers and shattered walls of ruined London. It was 1666 and the city had just been devastated by the Great Fire.

'What an opportunity!' muttered the man to himself. 'Now everything can be rebuilt in a beautiful, spacious way. There will be wide roads and leafy parks – no more of those crowded, unhealthy slums.'

So said Christopher Wren, a young architect, whose dreams of re-building London caused him to work day and night on the plans. Finally he finished and took his work to King Charles II.

'Marvellous,' exclaimed the king. 'Now we will have a city to be proud of; but first of all we'll have to get the rich merchants of the city to put up the money for the rebuilding.'

It was then that Christopher got his first shock.

'Far, far too expensive!' the merchants claimed. 'Out of the question.'

So what might have been a wonderful city disappeared before it got beyond the planning stage – but there was some consolation for Christopher Wren.

'You can plan and rebuild St Paul's Cathedral.'

On 21st June 1675, the first stone of the new cathedral was laid. For the next thirty-five years the building of the great cathedral was the life's work of Christopher Wren.

Finally, when he was seventy-eight years old, in 1710, the building was finished. Once a year after that the ailing architect was carried up to the top of the great dome to look out over the ever-growing London.

Was he disappointed that this was not being developed in the way he thought it should be? We will never know, but his own great work still stands proudly in his memory.

Information for the teacher

1 The October link for this story could be the date of birth of Sir Christopher Wren – 20th October, 1632. He was the son of the Dean of Windsor, chaplain to King Charles I. From childhood he showed great ability. He died on 25th February, 1723, and was buried ceremonially in St Paul's Cathedral. He was responsible for many other London buildings as well.

2 A possible Biblical link with this story is that of the Tower of Babel and why it failed (Genesis 11).

Hymn suggestion

Come and Praise Vol 2 'You can build a wall' No 91

Prayer

Let us give thanks this morning for the skill of men who have made the world a more beautiful place by their work. Let us think particularly of architects and builders whose work has to be so carefully planned and with so much attention to detail.

Let us also think of the designers and builders of religious buildings throughout the world. Amen.

National Curriculum cross-curricular reference

History provides a link here, dealing as it does in this case with a spectacular and fairly well-documented era. Science is equally obvious and any number of practical building experiments can be carried out by both individuals and groups. Plans and drawings would also involve Maths.

29   Akiba

Introduction

Do you sometimes find work at school hard? Is there a subject you never really seem to understand? This morning's story is about a man who found school work very hard indeed.

Story

Akiba fought to keep his eyes open. But the harder he tried the heavier his eyelids seemed to be.

'Oh, what's the use?' he thought. 'I'm just too tired for this reading business; after all, I do work all day.'

Akiba lived in Palestine and was a shepherd. He was tough and strong but he had never had the chance to learn to read and write. Then he met the beautiful Rachel.

Suddenly life changed and after a few weeks Akiba asked Rachel to marry him. Now Rachel came from a family where there were many books, and she knew what wonderful treasures they were.

'I will marry you, Akiba,' she said, 'on one condition.'

'What's that?' asked the poor shepherd.

'I know you've had a hard life,' went on Rachel, 'but I think it would be marvellous for you if you learned to read.'

'But . . . I'm nearly forty!' gasped the shepherd.

However, Rachel wouldn't change her mind until Akiba agreed. So after the wedding he went to see a rabbi. The rabbi agreed to teach Akiba to read. His lessons would be after his long days out in the fields with his sheep.

Akiba found it incredibly hard; he was always tired, he couldn't stay awake, and he just couldn't remember all the letters and sounds. So he decided he couldn't go on.

The day after having made his decision, he was out in the open air looking after his sheep when he came to a spring in the mountains. For some time he stood gazing at the little waterfall as it cascaded down on to the rock beneath. Then he looked even more closely at the rock and noticed the groove that had been worn in it by the water hitting it day after day after day. Akiba had a sudden thought.

'It's like reading,' he muttered to himself. 'If I keep on, and on, and on, like the waterfall, eventually *I will* be able to read.'

So Akiba went back to the rabbi and, putting his tiredness aside, he tried with even more determination. This time, not only did he learn to read, but he also began the journey which was to make him a very famous rabbi himself.

Information for the teacher

1 Akiba, after learning to read at forty, ultimately became one of the foremost authorities on the Torah (the Jewish law). He lived during the Roman occupation of Palestine and was executed in his nineties for refusing to obey an order from the Romans which forbade the study of the Torah.
2 This story could be linked with the Jewish festival of Simchat Torah (the Rejoicing of the Law) which takes place on 23rd of Tishri, a link with October.
3 A useful address here is: The Jewish Education Bureau, 8 Westcombe Avenue, Leeds LS8 2BS.

Hymn suggestion

Come and Praise Vol 2 'You can build a wall' No 91

Prayer

Let us think this morning about the quality of determination. Without it we cannot succeed when things get difficult. Let us remember that in everybody's life there are good times and bad times and to deal with the last of these we often need determination and persistence.

We pray that we might be given the strength of character to be determined in times of difficulty.

National Curriculum cross-curricular reference

Science could be well served by investigations into the wearing effects of water and weather. This could include outside observation and controlled experiments within the classroom.

Music could be involved in experimenting with, and assessing the need for persistence, in mastering a song, or a simple piece of music on tuned percussion.

30 Sending a message

Introduction

If we want to give somebody who lives a long way away a message, we can telephone them or send them a letter. Sending messages wasn't always this easy.

Story

Johnny urged his horse to go even faster. His heart pounded as the galloping hooves flashed over the barren desert ground. His clothes were drenched with sweat in the 100°F heat, but all he could think about were the Indians behind him. Occasionally an arrow whistled over his head and he could hear the cries and shouts as the party of Indians urged their horses to even greater speed.

'Come on, Beauty, come on,' whispered Johnny to his gallant horse – and gradually the gap between him and his pursuers widened. Eventually they gave up the chase.

No sooner had they done so than a bolt of lightning flashed across the sky, to be followed by a huge clap of thunder. The massive rain drops hit Johnny like small stones and soon the first rain for months was drenching horse and rider.

Gritting his teeth, fifteen-year-old Johnny kept his horse going flat out. He had seventy-six miles to cover and he must do it fast!

The year was 1860 and Johnny was a rider for the American Pony Express. This was an organisation which used young riders, who didn't weigh much, to carry mail two thousand miles across the USA. They galloped at top speed from staging post to staging post where they changed horses. Their journeys took them through desert heat, mountain snow, hostile Indian country and areas of marauding bands of outlaws. Riders faced injury and death every time they mounted a horse.

Johnny survived all his rides and lived for many years to tell of his adventures. The reason for this was that, in October 1861, engineers finished hooking up telegraph wires from the east coast to the west coast of America. Now a message could be sent in less time than it took to saddle one of the Pony Express horses!

Information for the teacher

1 The Pony Express lasted for only eighteen months, but during its existence 650,000 miles were covered by its young riders. It was founded by Senator William Gavin of California, because delivery of mail by stage coach was slow and unreliable.
2 The maximum weight riders were allowed to be was 9st. 10lbs. They carried their documents in a pouch called a mochilla.
3 The most famous Pony Express rider was William Cody who was later to achieve worldwide fame as Buffalo Bill.

Hymn suggestion

Come and Praise Vol 1 'One more step' No 47

Prayer

Dear God, Thank you for the skill of men whose inventions have saved lives. Let us be grateful that today we can send a message without endangering lives as was once the case.

We give thanks for this progress made in our modern world. Amen.

National Curriculum cross-curricular reference

There is a great deal of scope for English work here: drama, writing 'first hand' accounts of rides, writing advertisements to persuade young riders to join the Pony Express.

This work can be linked to a study of some of the routes across the USA, noting distances, varied climate and terrain.

In a wider Religious Education context this could fit into one of the 'different aspects of courage' considerations.

November

31 The friend

Introduction

There is an old saying: 'A friend in need is a friend indeed'. This morning's story shows us exactly what that saying means.

Story

Damon and Pythias were very good friends. They did as much as they could together and always enjoyed each other's company. They lived in a city called Syracuse and the man who ruled it was cruel and ruthless. His name was Dionysus.

Damon said to Pythias, 'That Dionysus is not fit to rule this great city. Somebody else should have the job.'

'It's dangerous to go round saying things like that,' replied Pythias. 'You want to be careful.'

But Damon wasn't careful. Finally he was arrested and taken before Dionysus.

'You'd like to get rid of me, I hear,' said the ruler, 'so you must be a dangerous man to have around.' With a wave of his hand Dionysus summoned two of his soldiers. 'Throw this wretch in prison. He dies in three days.'

Damon was shocked but not surprised at these dreadful words. Bowing his head, he asked Dionysus if he could say farewell to his family before the execution. They lived a day's journey away.

Dionysus stared at his prisoner for a while, and then a sly grin came over his face. 'Yes,' he said finally. 'You can do that – but Pythias must take your place whilst you are away. If you're not back in three days he dies in your place.'

Secretly Dionysus thought that this was a wonderful idea. He was sure Damon would not return. Then he would kill Pythias, another trouble maker, and after that send his soldiers to find and kill Damon. In this way he would get rid of both men.

So Damon left the city and Pythias took his place in prison.

After saying a tearful farewell to his family, Damon called for his horse to return to Syracuse.

'It's gone, sir,' said his servant.

'Gone? Gone? What do you mean?'

'I sold it . . . now you can't return to die . . . you can stay here and . . .'

Damon looked at his kind old servant, then without a word, he turned and began to run back to Syracuse. After hours of desperate effort he was tired, dirty and knew that he could never reach the city in time. Then he saw a man with a horse. Giving the stranger every penny he possessed he leapt on the horse and galloped on his way.

Meanwhile, back in Syracuse the deadline had been reached. Dionysus stood smiling in front of a group of soldiers. Amongst them knelt Pythias, who was about to be beheaded.

'So much for friends,' smirked Dionysus, when suddenly a horse pounded into the courtyard and Damon threw himself down from it.

'My friend,' he cried, rushing up to Pythias, 'thank goodness I'm in time!'

Dionysus was dumbfounded.

'You've come back,' he gasped.

'Wait,' he went on as the soldiers closed in on the two friends. 'This is really true friendship. Neither of you will be hurt – and I hope I can learn from your example. Perhaps then I might be called a friend of yours too.'

Information for the teacher

1 A useful Biblical link is the story of David and Jonathan (Samuel 1, 18–20).
2 Damon's actions were certainly 'saintly' and some further follow-ups could be linked with All Saints Day on 1st November.
3 The story of Damon, Pythias and Dionysus is a traditional Greek legend. Many more can be found in the chapter: 'Myths and Legends of the Greeks' which is contained in *The Encyclopaedia of Myths and Legends of all Nations* by Robinson and Wilson (Kaye and Ward).

Hymn suggestion

Come and Praise Vol 1 'A man for all the people' No 27

Prayer

Let us think this morning about keeping our word, no matter how difficult this may be. Let us remember that promises are made to be kept and we should never say we will do something unless we really mean to. Let us also give thanks for loyal friends everywhere.

National Curriculum cross-curricular reference

In both History and Geography links can be made with this story of ancient Greece.

32 Happiness

Introduction

Let us spend half a minute in absolute silence thinking about things which make us really happy . . . now listen to this morning's story.

Story

Ghandar had one great aim in life.

'If only I had one of those magnificent silk-lined cloaks,' he thought to himself. 'Then everybody would see how rich and important I have become.'

Now Ghandar made his money by buying things cheaply and selling them expensively. He also worked hard and spent all his time earning money. He had no wife or children, nor any real friends – he hadn't time for such things.

Well, of course, he got rich and the great moment came when he chose his cloak. It really was magnificent. It was purple and, as everyone knew, that was the most expensive colour anybody could have. It was huge and almost wrapped round Ghandar twice. Its lining was of the finest silk and it fastened with a precious stone.

'Fantastic,' thought Ghandar, 'what happiness, what a wonderful cloak. How other people must admire and envy me.'

At home that night Ghandar didn't take his cloak off once. He stroked it and fingered it and smoothed it over his arms.

'Wonderful,' he kept muttering.

Finally, after hanging his cloak up very carefully, he went to bed. That night whilst he was asleep a thief broke into his house and stole the cloak.

When he awoke and found his precious cloak had gone Ghandar was heartbroken. All that money he had spent so much time earning so that he could buy the cloak – all that and the cloak – gone. Now he had nothing.

In the same town lived a young man called Bhattabhatika. At about the time Ghandar was discovering his loss, Bhattabhatika was preparing to leave home to go and seek his fortune in the world.

'Mother,' he said, 'what shall I do to find happiness in the world?'

His mother smiled. 'What you do doesn't matter as much as how you do it,' she said. 'Always do your best and treat everybody you meet with kindness and consideration. That's the way to find happiness.'

Information for the teacher

1 A very useful Bible reference here is Matthew 6, 19–21.
2 The Buddha's teaching was that the ideal state of Nirvana could only be reached through kindliness, compassion and the joy of inner peace.
3 A useful calendar link with this story is that 2nd November is the anniversary of the founding of the Samaritans in 1953. 'Giving to those in need' can be explored in various themes.

Hymn suggestion

Come and Praise Vol 2 'I come like a beggar' No 90

Prayer

> Let us try to be:
> Loving instead of angry
> Kind instead of greedy,
> Truthful instead of deceitful.
> Let us try and remember
> That we gain the most
> By giving the most. (Adapted from Buddhist scriptures)

National Curriculum cross-curricular reference

Science, Geography and History can all be involved in a further study of clothes – what, where and when.

33 *What are you good at?*

Introduction

What are you good at? It might be playing football or whistling; painting or telling good jokes; mending bikes or making mince pies! Whatever it is, by doing something well you will not only give yourself a lot of pleasure, but other people too . . . even if you are not quite as clever as Felix was.

Story

'How does he do it?' people used to say.

'Have you seen him ride a horse? Brilliant, that's all I can say.'

'And what a sportsman, he can run like the wind.'

'What about all those languages he can speak – he must be a really clever fellow.'

'And play the piano – not just the old songs and tunes, but all those brilliant new ones he writes himself.'

Felix was used to hearing admiring comments about himself. It was true he was a good sportsman, and he was very clever and he had been able to play the piano since he was a small child. From the age of fourteen he began to write wonderful music too.

One day someone asked him the secret of his success. 'Ah,' replied Felix, 'I don't know about success, but I am happy and this is because I really do enjoy working hard at whatever I am doing.'

Because Felix was not only a very clever person but also someone who was prepared to work hard, we can still listen to the marvellous music he wrote.

Information for the teacher

1 Felix Mendelssohn Bartholdy died on 4th November 1847 at the age of thirty-eight.
2 The playing of some of his music at this assembly would obviously enhance it. Two suggested choices might be something evocative ('Fingal's Cave') or something familiar ('The Wedding March'). The latter is on one of those very useful compilations: 'The Music Masters' EMI SPR 90049.
3 For top juniors, more food for thought could stem from the fact that because he was Jewish, Mendelssohn's music was banned during the Nazi rule of Germany.

Hymn suggestion

Come and Praise Vol 2 'Sing people sing' No 110

Prayer

Thank you God for talents and senses. Thank you for enabling us to hear great music and thank you for the talent given to those who write and play it.

National Curriculum cross-curricular reference

In Music some further study of the effect of music on movement might be considered: 'The Wedding March', for example, invites what kind of movement? What music is appropriate for quick, lively, slow, sad movement? With some advance preparation and collection of varied musical examples much interesting work can be done here.

34 John and Errol

Introduction

If you have ever been in hospital you will know what a difference it makes to meet somebody there who is always cheerful.

Story

One day John woke up and he couldn't open his eyes. He was very frightened. He rubbed them and they felt swollen and sore. He couldn't get them to open and he couldn't see.

'Mum,' he cried out, '*MUM!*'

Hearing his frightened cry, John's mother rushed into his bedroom. 'What is it . . . oh dear.'

Soon the doctor arrived to see if he could help. 'I think I know what the problem is,' he said, 'but it will take time to get things put right. Meanwhile John will have to go to hospital.'

Later that day John was lying in bed in the local hospital. He was very miserable and frightened. He couldn't control his muffled sobs.

'What's the matter?' asked a voice.

John knew that the voice belonged to the boy who was in the next bed. The nurse had told him there were only two of them in the room.

'I can't see,' said John . . . 'and I'm scared.'

'Don't worry,' replied the other boy in a cheerful tone. 'My name is Errol and I'll soon cheer you up. I'm only in here 'cos I broke my leg.'

Soon the two boys were talking together.

'What's it like in here?' asked John.

'What do you mean?' asked Errol.

'Well . . . what it looks like . . . and everything.'

There was a very long pause.

'Errol? Did you hear what I said?' asked John.

'Oh . . . yeah . . . yeah. Well it's . . . sort of very bright. The door is bright yellow, the curtains have got big flowers on them and the nurse is very pretty. There's lots of things you can see through the window too.'

'Tell me some more,' whispered John.

For the next few days Errol kept cheering John up with his tales of what he could see going on all around – how the nurse looked, what the weather was like, kinds of cars he could see outside and so on. His constant cheery chatter made John forget about his eyes until . . . one morning he woke . . . and he could see again!

'Errol!' he cried. 'Errol . . . I can see . . . I can *see*!'

'Oh . . . that's great John, really great.'

'Now you won't have to keep telling me about things I can see for mys . . .'

Suddenly John stopped talking as he looked round. There were no low windows in this room . . . the door was a dark brown colour . . . there were no flowery curtains . . .

John looked across at Errol, who had a plaster cast on his leg but was sitting up in bed and staring straight ahead . . . with sightless eyes.

'OK, OK,' said Errol, 'now you know. Well I had to cheer you up, didn't I? And I *have* got a broken leg. Now – you can tell me what it's like in here!'

Information for the teacher

1 A strong November link in the 'those who care for us' theme relates to 5th November 1855, the date when Florence Nightingale arrived in Scutari. For those who want to pursue the sight aspect, then Louis Braille was born on 4th January 1809.

2 Two addresses which might be useful are:

Guide Dogs for the Blind, 9–11 Park Street, Windsor, Berks. SL4 1JR.

Royal National Institute for the Blind, 224 Great Portland Street, London W1.

Hymn suggestion

Come and Praise Vol 1 'From the darkness came light' No 29

Prayer

Dear God, Teach us to be thankful for our senses. Help us to use them as fully as we can to enjoy so much that is beautiful in the world.

Please help those unfortunate people who are handicapped in some way and cannot enjoy all their senses as we do. Amen.

National Curriculum cross-curricular reference

Science, in the context of 'health' or 'handicaps' or 'our bodies', is one link here and this could be linked to History in terms of improved medical care, etc.

Both Religious Education and Geography are routes to developing the theme in a Third World context and 'senses' offers varied possibilities in Music, PE and English.

35 Know your strengths

Introduction

It is very easy to be flattered. For instance somebody might say to you 'You are a really lovely singer', when you know you are not. But perhaps when this is said, you start to believe it. Now in this morning's story . . .

Story

The pale moon shone down over the field. The shadows of the trees and hedges sharpened and blurred as scattered clouds scudded across the sky. One shadow moved. Slowly and carefully it crept and stopped and edged forwards. The wolf was closing in on his prey.

The shepherd and his dogs slept, the sheep and lambs huddled close to each other. The wolf got nearer. He had spotted a lamb on the outside of the flock. Stealthily he moved towards it, and then with a fierce swoop he had it in his jaws and was dragging it off to a nearby hill where he could enjoy his supper.

Awake and terrified, the lamb realised she was in terrible danger.

'Mr Wolf, Mr Wolf,' she cried, as the wolf surged strongly up the slope of the hill. Keeping the lamb firmly in his jaws the wolf simply growled.

'Mr Wolf,' went on the lamb, 'I know you've caught me fair and square . . . but . . . please . . . one last request before I die.'

'This is a very strange lamb,' thought the wolf, but his curiosity was aroused. Stopping on his upward path, he relaxed his savage jaws and snarled.

'What is it then?'

'Well . . .' went on the lamb, 'one of my great regrets – if I am to die – is that I have never heard your voice.'

'What do you mean?'

'My parents told me so much about you – not only are you fierce and strong and independent – but you also have such a wonderful singing voice.'

'A what?' muttered the surprised wolf.

'All the flock knows about it. They might be terrified of you, but they also know what a marvellous singer you are. They've heard you. Please, before you eat me – will you sing just one short song?'

'I . . .' the wolf was flattered.

Putting one paw firmly on the lamb he threw back his head and began to howl, long and loud.

Instantly the shepherd and the guard dogs were awakened. Recognising the wolf's howl and fearing for the flock, they raced towards the sound.

Far from being his usual cautious, crafty self the wolf, with his eyes closed, continued to lift his head in 'song'. With a rush the dogs were on him. Bruised and cut he managed to fight them off and dash away safely up the hill.

Finally, when the shepherd, dogs and rescued lamb returned to the flock he sat, panting and sore, looking down on them. He had learnt a lesson tonight.

Information for the teacher

1 A possible November link for this story could be the fact that Peter Tchaikovsky, the Russian composer, died on 6th November, 1893. 'Peter and the Wolf' would be very evocative music to introduce and conclude the assembly.

2 A Biblical story which conveys the theme of flattery undoing strength is Samson and Delilah. It can be found in Judges 16.

3 For older children this theme could be developed one stage further – what motivation do people often have when they say flattering things about a person, or an object (a car they want to sell for instance)? This could obviously lead on to areas like honesty and would provide good discussion material for Year 6 children.

Hymn suggestion

Come and Praise Vol 2 ' 'Tis the gift to be simple' No 97

Prayer

Dear God, Give us the wisdom to know ourselves. Let us not be deceived by false words. Help us to be honest with ourselves and others. Amen.

National Curriculum cross-curricular reference

This assembly story lends itself very readily to drama, thus involving English. Its dramatic impact would be greatly enhanced by some simple 'composed' music, thus fulfilling one of the criteria of National Curriculum Music.

It is also a good theme for artistic work and the historical and geographical aspects of shepherds and sheep could be followed up.

36 The determined friends

Introduction

One of the best things about having a really good friend is knowing that he, or she, will always help you if you are in trouble.

Story

The sun was burning down. The four men were desperately hot and their shoulders ached from carrying the fifth man, who lay on a stretcher.

'Not long now,' said Timothy.

'No,' agreed Philip. 'I can just about see the houses of Capernaum from here.'

'We'll soon be there, old friend,' went on John, as he leaned forward to wipe the sweat from the brow of the sick man who lay on the stretcher.

Timothy, John, Philip and Thomas were four of a group of five close friends. The fifth friend, Abraham, was ill and the others were concerned about him. Timothy had heard that there was this man called Jesus, who was travelling round the countryside and doing wonderful things for sick people. He had suggested to the others that they carry Abraham to the nearby town of Capernaum which Jesus was visiting. He was sure Jesus would be able to help Abraham. After several hours of walking in the scorching heat they were nearly there.

'Look,' said Philip, 'he must be in that house over on the right. There's a huge crowd of people gathered round it.'

'It could be tricky getting through that lot,' muttered John doubtfully.

'We'll manage!' was Thomas's firm and confident answer.

Eventually the group reached the huge crowd gathered round one of Capernaum's larger houses.

'You can't get through here,' somebody shouted to the four stretcher bearers.

'Well just let us try, will you?' urged Timothy as the four friends struggled with the stretcher.

After half an hour of pushing and squeezing the group reached the door leading into the house. Then they finally came to a halt. The passage and room inside the house were absolutely packed with people standing shoulder to shoulder. It was impossible for even one more person to squeeze in, never mind four men with a stretcher.

Gasping with the efforts they had made the four disappointed men heard the voice of Jesus from inside the house. Abraham lay motionless on the stretcher. Suddenly Philip began gazing at the flight of open steps which led up to the roof of the house.

'I've got an idea!' he said suddenly. 'Come on, up here.'

As the friends eased the stretcher up the steps Philip explained: 'Right, now listen. These steps will take us up to the roof. The roof itself it only made of sticks and dried mud – so it will be easy to make a hole in it, and repair it afterwards. Once we have made a hole we can take the cords off our tunics. If we tie one to each of the four corners of the stretcher we can lower it through the hole – down to Jesus who will be underneath.'

A few minutes later the people crowded into the large room wondered what was happening when bits of the roof began to drop down. A very short time later the stretcher appeared and began to come down towards Jesus – the determined friends had succeeded!

Information for the teacher

1 1st November is All Saints Day, when people who gave much, or all, for the benefit of others are especially remembered.

The idea of 'four good friends' could be perpetuated by the story of the four Christian stone masons who together refused to carve a pagan statue for the Emperor Diocletian. He had them put to death for their refusal and the Feast Day in their memory is 8th November.

On 22nd of the month, in 1906, the international distress call 'Mayday' was universally accepted. It comes from the French *m'aider* or 'Help me.'

2 Teachers may wish to go on and finish this story from its Biblical origins. For those wishing to do so the source is: Mark 2, 1–12.

3 Biblical stories are always enhanced by background knowledge and one excellent source for this is *The Book of the Bible – An Encyclopaedic Guide to the World's Greatest Book* (Purnell).

Hymn suggestion

Come and Praise Vol 1 'A man for all the people' No 27

Prayer

Dear God, Give us the determination to overcome disappointment and discouragement by your guidance and example. Teach us to value friendship and be grateful for the love and care of our friends. Amen.

National Curriculum cross-curricular reference

There are possibilities of linking practical CDT work to this story and both Science and Geography could be involved in location of the events, climatic conditions, effects and requirements of such a climate, etc.

Religious Education could be extended into looking at other examples of friendship given in the Bible, the most obvious example being David and Jonathan (Samuel 1, Chapters 18, 19, 20).

37 *This month*

Introduction

> No sun, no moon,
> No morn, no noon,
> No dawn, no dusk, no proper time of day . . .
> . . . November. (Thomas Hood)

This month

The whole of Thomas Hood's poem about November paints it as a gloomy, dark month with little good about it.

This, however, is not true. Whilst the trees which are not evergreens will have shed most of their leaves, this gives us an opportunity to see birds much more closely. There are plenty of birds still about too. Few of them are singing but the robin is an exception and his song can be heard frequently.

Flocks of birds are much easier to spot and groups of magpies and starlings are common at this time of the year. Squirrels are still about on milder days and when they are hungry. Woods are carpeted in leaves of the most lovely colours still and there are plenty of fungi on show.

Despite the fogs and mists of the month other things to look for are Old Man's Beard, and juniper, an evergreen shrub.

The Anglo-Saxons had two names for November, these were Winmonath and Blodmonath. The first was because cold winds often blew at this time; the second meant 'blood month' because this was the time when cattle were killed to provide winter food.

There are lots of weather predictions associated with November. For instance, if the wind is in the south-west on St Martin's Day (11th), it is supposed to stay there right through to Candlemas in February and make sure we have a mild winter.

So despite its miserable reputation November is still a month with lots of interest in the natural world around us.

Information for the teacher

1 Balancing the rather restricted activity of being outside in November is a whole list of things useful for children's interest – Guy Fawkes' Day; the Lord Mayor of London's Show; Armistice Day; St Cecilia's Day (22nd), (Cecilia is the patron saint of music);

St Catherine's Day (25th). Catherine was a Christian girl who in the fourth century refused to give up her religion.

2 A useful piece of information which could be projected in a 'working together' theme and linked to this assembly, concerns starlings. Large flocks of them can be seen flying over the countryside at this time of the year. The birds at the rear who are feeding then fly over the birds ahead of them to scan the ground below. The process is continually repeated so that there are always some of the birds searching for food below, and no ground is therefore neglected.

Hymn suggestion

Come and Praise Vol 1 'Think of a world without any flowers' No 17

Prayer

Let us think this morning about those countries where the climate causes distress to people. Let us pray that all people might have sufficient warmth, food and homes to be comfortable. Amen.

National Curriculum cross-curricular reference

Science is the obvious choice here, particularly with regard to environmental matters. Geography too could be involved and there are strong descriptive writing opportunities in English.

38 Not so useless

Introduction

All of us like to laugh – but none of us likes to be laughed at. This morning's story starts with some cruel laughter.

Story

The lion, the elephant and the tiger all roared with laughter. The sound, rumbling from their deep chests, shook the leaves on the trees.

'You're useless,' growled the lion, 'you can't do anything.'

Anansi, the spider, listened to the laughter with bowed head.

'It's true,' twittered the birds flying overhead, 'you can't fight, fly, swim . . .'

'. . . even run fast,' murmured the deer.

Anansi looked round at all the other animals in the forest and began to speak.

'I'm not useless, I'll . . .'

'You'll what?' snarled the tiger.

'I'll . . . I'll . . . capture the snake. That'll show you who is useless!'

For a moment there was silence. Nobody laughed or joked about the snake – they were too scared of him. Then there was a chorus of catcalls from the animals.

'Capture the snake? Impossible.'

'He'll finish you off in the flick of an eyelid.'

'Bah!'

'Prove it.'

An hour later Anansi was alone. What had he let himself in for? He had no idea how he was going to capture the snake – or had he?

The next day Anansi sat outside the snake's house. When the bushes parted and the snake came sliding out Anansi shivered at the sight of the long, strong, cold-eyed creature. The snake ignored Anansi, went in search of food and returned home.

The same thing happened for the next few days. Eventually the snake stopped and fixed Anansi with his cold, cruel eyes.

'Every morning when I come out you are sitting there watching me, Anansi. It's beginning to annoy me, and when I get annoyed somebody had better watch out!'

'Oh the last thing I want to do is annoy you, Mr Snake,' said Anansi respectfully. 'No, no, certainly not, but . . . well . . . you see . . .'

'Come on – out with it.'

'Well, the animals have been arguing about who is the longest creature in the forest. Of course I said it was you but the others all reckon the crocodile is . . .'

'I am the longest,' replied the snake curtly.

'Of course, of course, no doubt, I know,' stuttered Anansi, 'but it's proving it, you see. I've been plucking up courage to ask you.'

'Ask me what?'

'Well – could I possibly measure you, Mr Snake?'

'How are you going to do that?'

'Look at this bamboo pole, Mr Snake.' Anansi pointed to the pole lying on the ground. 'If you lie beside it I can mark off your measurements.'

The snake sighed and gave Anansi a baleful look.

'All right – if it will prove to those fools who is the longest.'

The snake stretched out alongside the bamboo pole. Anansi fussed around the pole, pushing it closer to the snake's body.

'Oh dear.'

'What's the matter?'

'Well when you press your head against the pole your tail moves away.'

'Tie my tail to the end then.'

Quickly Anansi tied the snake's tail firmly to the bamboo. 'Now, Mr Snake, could you really stretch out please?'

Keen now to be measured at his longest, the snake stretched fully, closing his eyes with the effort.

Anansi, scarcely able to breathe at his daring, snapped a rope round the snake's head and, in a flash, tied him to the bamboo. Two more pieces of rope secured his body in the middle.

No sooner had the snake been captured in this way than a passing bird saw him. News flashed round the forest in minutes.

The snake was captured! Anansi had done it. From that day on Anansi was never considered useless again.

Information for the teacher

1 Anansi is a cultural hero in West Africa. There are legions of stories about how his trickery more than compensates for his lack of strength. His fame is equally great in the West Indies.

For teachers seeking original assembly material then *African Myths and Legends* by K. Arnott (Oxford University Press) is a useful collection. Many of the stories emphasise such qualities as a sense of justice, patience and endurance.

2 There are two November connections which form links with the core material for this assembly.

3rd November is National Day in Dominica, West Indies and Panama.

Sir John Hawkins, the British sailor who died in the West Indies on 12 November 1595, took the first negro slaves to these islands.

Hymn suggestion

Come and Praise Vol 1 'All creatures of our God and King' No 7

Prayer

Dear God, Let us enjoy the pleasure of laughter together. Teach us to laugh with people and not at them. Help us to value the qualities and talents of everyone we know. Amen.

National Curriculum cross-curricular reference

Much relevant English work, both oral and written, comes from telling stories in the manner of this assembly tale. These can be closely linked with drama, and older children could be encouraged to try and create new characters.

Geographically it may be useful to locate areas where Anansi stories are popular.

39   The beggar

Introduction

It is easy to give presents to people we know well and like. It is more difficult to give to strangers, particularly if what we give is something we very much want to keep for ourselves.

Story

The wind whistled round the line of soldiers as they made their way across the bleak countryside to the city in the distance.

'I'll be glad to be inside in front of a warm fire,' said one.

'Me too,' agreed his companion.

The soldiers were Romans and they were on duty in Gaul. Each was well equipped and had a thick cloak to keep out the biting wind.

As they reached the city gate they heard a moaning sound above the noise of the wind.

'Help me . . . please . . . food . . . anything.'

The moans and pleas came from a beggar. Dressed in filthy rags, he lay on the ground beside the city gate. As the soldiers drew nearer he increased his begging cries.

'What a welcome!' muttered one Roman.

'You're going to catch cold lying there,' shouted another.

'Maybe he's too warm inside,' snorted a third.

There was a roar of laughter from the group, and one of the soldiers moved over to give the beggar a kick as he walked past.

But one of the Romans didn't feel the same as the others. 'That poor, miserable man,' he thought. 'How desperately cold and poor he must be. If only I had something to give him.'

But as the soldier, whose name was Martin, fingered his empty purse he knew that he had nothing . . . or had he?

'Yes,' he thought suddenly. Stopping beside the beggar, he unfastened his thick cloak at the neck and swept it off his shoulders. With a stroke from his sword he cut it in two.

Then, carefully, he wrapped one half round the shivering man. When he had done this he shrugged into what was left of his cloak and hurried to catch up with his colleagues.

The other soldiers looked at him in amazement, said nothing and avoided his eye.

Soon they were inside the city and warmed by food and shelter. With the others Martin lay down to sleep. It seemed that his head had hardly touched the pillow when he began to dream.

In his dream Martin saw the half of his cloak which he had torn and given away. It was no longer being worn by a beggar, it was wrapped round the shoulders of a man Martin recognised as Jesus. As the dream continued Martin thought he could hear Jesus telling a group of people round him how he had been given the cloak.

With a start the soldier awoke. He lay in the darkness trying to collect his thoughts. Then he sat up. 'I've got work to do,' he said to himself.

Shortly after this he left the army and became a monk. For many years he travelled round Gaul, preaching about Jesus and helping people in any way he could. Finally he settled in the city of Tours and became a bishop there.

When he died in 397, Martin had become famous for his concern for, and kindness to, others. He is especially remembered every year on 11th November and many churches are named after him.

Information for the teacher

1 Martin was born in Hungary where his father was a Roman soldier. Following in his father's footsteps he too became a soldier at the age of fifteen. It is thought that the famous incident described here took place when he was about eighteen.

2 There may well be a St Martin's Church known to the children locally. Probably the most famous one in England is St Martin's-in-the-Fields in London.

3 A useful book, with a section on 'The Christians' which contains the stories of several saints, is *Heroes of the Faith* by William Dargue (Oxford University Press).

Hymn suggestion

Come and Praise Vol 2 'I come like a beggar' No 90

Prayer

Let us think this morning about the following words:

> We love our friends
> That is easy.
> Let us learn to love others
> Near and far,
> Known and unknown to us.
> Let us learn that
> What hurts them also hurts us.
> Teach us to share
> All that we have
> With those who have nothing.
> (Adapted from an original African prayer)

National Curriculum cross-curricular reference

The Roman Empire is a recommended Junior School theme and this story can be used to focus attention on specific aspects of it: the growth of Christianity during its existence – how, where, and with what consequences.

The recognition of Gaul/France in an atlas could lead to studying the geographical aspects of the Roman Empire.

Some Science and CDT work can be done on practical considerations of materials and clothes which keep us warm.

40 War and peace

Introduction
Dreadful things happen in wartime, but sometimes strange events and acts of kindness take place too.

Story

Bullets whistled overhead as Lieutenant Paul George, a vet, ran crouching along the muddy trench during a day's action in the First World War. English and German soldiers faced each other in hundreds of miles of trenches. From time to time huge shells dropped on either side and threw up great mounds of earth. There was never any peace from the rifle and machine gun fire.

Then, above the hideous noise, Lieutenant George heard a pitiful whining. Turning a corner in the trench he saw a German Shepherd dog lying on its side, bleeding from a wound.

'Now old chap, we'll soon fix this up,' he said as he bent over the dog. For the next few minutes the vet cleaned and bandaged the wound as the dog gratefully licked his hand.

Lieutenant George knew that both sides used dogs to carry messages but he got a surprise when he looked at the wounded dog's collar and saw '1826 Karl' – it was obviously a dog used by the Germans.

Looking down at his patient, Lieutenant George knew that the dog needed further careful treatment and that he would be better getting it where he felt at home. The vet came to a decision.

Putting his hands to his mouth the lieutenant shouted at the top of his voice: '1826 Karl'. There was a slight pause in the gunfire and he took advantage of this to shout again: '1826 Karl – to come home'.

This time the firing ceased all together.

Lieutenant George stood up and climbed out of the trench with the wounded dog following him painfully. The two of them stood there in No Man's Land with hundreds of eyes watching them and dozens of guns stilled.

Speaking gently, Lieutenant George patted the dog and sent him limping and bandaged on his way to the German lines.

A week later, under cloudy skies, the noise of gunfire rolled again over the long trenches. Then, suddenly, there came a cry from the German lines: '1826 Karl'. There was a lessening of the fire, and the shout came again: '1826 Karl'.

This time every gun stopped. There was sudden complete silence. It was as if hundreds of men were holding their breath. Then, slowly, from out of the German trenches there climbed a dog handler. After him climbed a fit and healthy Karl. The German soldier bent down and put a leash on Karl, then carefully he walked the fully recovered dog for a hundred yards between the lines of trenches.

The silence lasted for perhaps a minute longer, and then it was broken by the first cheer. Suddenly the air was full of the sound of cheers, clapping hands and whistles. Those tired, battle-weary men were giving thanks that one dog had been restored to fitness and health.

Information for the teacher

1 This assembly could be used on, or near, Remembrance Day, 11th November. Just one of the many dreadful statistics of the First World War: eight million five hundred thousand soldiers were killed during the fighting.

2 A very evocative piece of prose written by a twelve-year-old boy could be used in connection with thoughts on the distress caused by war:

'When they dropped the atom bomb there was a terrible explosion and a terrifically strong blast. People were blown against trees and buildings. When it was over only shadows were left in the slight breeze.' (Originally published in *Assembly* by Redvers Brandling (Macmillan))

3 Some thoughtful work could be done on the 'bitter sweet' popular songs associated with the First World War – 'Goodbyee', 'It's a long way to Tipperary', etc.

Suggested hymn

Come and Praise Vol 1 'Peace, perfect peace' No 53

Prayer

Dear God, Please give men wisdom that they might forever be without war. Teach us to avoid the faults which cause argument and distress. Help us to be free from greed, selfishness and prejudice. Amen.

National Curriculum cross-curricular reference

Wars and their causes offer many opportunities for History work for upper juniors, while locating the areas of conflict incorporates Geography.

The Music aspect could go beyond the First World War popular songs to more examples of songs about war and peace.

41 A life-saving swim

Introduction

If we look carefully enough at our daily papers we can usually find stories of very brave people. One November day all the papers told the following story.

Story

'I can't hold her much longer – we're going in.'

The pilot of the twin-engined Piper Seneca plane called out desperately to his passengers as he struggled with the controls. Using all his skill he managed to level the plane out before it hit the sea with a bone-shattering crash.

'OK – everybody out – as quickly as possible!' shouted pilot Brad Youngberg. Surprisingly no one was hurt and as their aircraft sank they kicked around in the water.

'Right,' spluttered Brad. 'I'm sure somebody must have seen us go in.'

But he was wrong, and soon he and the others, Dan Tuckfield, Delano Hicks, Ira and Dorothy Bloom, realised that their situation was desperate.

They had crashed off the coast of Florida in the USA, and twenty-five miles away the resort of Cat Cay was their nearest land. They had no dinghy or raft and their only hope was to swim the twenty-five miles.

It was then that Dan Tuckfield began organising things.

'You two,' he said to Brad and Delano, who were good swimmers, 'get going. I'll help the others.'

So Dan began to swim to the shore. Dorothy Bloom couldn't swim so Dan carried her on his back. Ira was such a poor swimmer that he had to hang on to Dan by a strap.

For hour after hour the small party struggled through the sea. As they did so tiger sharks hovered nearby, waiting to pounce.

All through the night the survivors swam on, with Dan doing the swimming for three people. When morning came the Blooms could go on no longer. They had both swallowed a lot of salt water and one after the other they died and slipped beneath the waves.

Don, Brad and Delano had now been swimming for more than twenty-four hours and Dan could see that the other two were almost ready to give up too.

'Don't stop,' he gasped. 'You must . . . *must* . . . keep going.'

Agonisingly slowly the land got nearer.

'Listen,' Dan called, 'I'm going to swim ahead and get help. All you've got to do is stay afloat until help arrives.'

With the last drop of his remaining strength Dan struck out strongly for the shore. When he reached it he staggered to the road where he saw a man walking. Hardly able to speak he gasped out his plea for help.

Soon a helicopter was roaring out to sea to pick up the other two exhausted men. Without Dan's courage and determination they would certainly have died too. He had swum the full twenty-five miles and it had taken him thirty-eight hours to do it.

'I'm sorry I couldn't save the other two,' he said later.

Information for the teacher

1 This story appeared on 16th November 1991. The party had been flying from Fort Lauderdale to the Bahamas when the crash occurred.
2 There is a natural link between this story and the other November feature 'Cold and Alone'. Both emphasise qualities of determination and resourcefulness.
3 An appropriate quotation from the Bible might be: 'A faithful friend is a secure shelter' (Ecclesiasticus 6, 14).

Hymn suggestion

Come and Praise Vol 1 'The journey of life' No 45

Prayer

Let us bow our heads and think this morning about those people who, by their courage, determination, strength and skill, save the lives of others. Let us pray that in time of need we might have the same qualities to help ourselves and others. Amen.

National Curriculum cross-curricular reference

Locating the scene of the story would be a useful geographical exercise and Science might be embraced in considering powered flight (and reasons for its failure), as well as health, exercise, swimming.

In English a useful discussion could involve the children in speculating about the exact steps which must have taken place from the time Dan staggered up the beach to the helicopter delivering the other two survivors to hospital.

42 *A long tongue makes for a short life*

Introduction

The Armenian proverb which is the title of this morning's story is one to make us think. It could be linked to another wise saying: 'Actions speak louder than words'.

Story

Long ago a fox, a wolf and a camel were making a long journey together. They had become friends, but the journey was long and tiring and they were often hungry. One day as they trudged along, the camel, who was much taller than the other two, saw something lying on the trail ahead.

'Something lying on the ground up there,' he said in his usual terse way.

'I wonder what it can be?' said the fox excitedly.

'Let's hurry up and find out,' added the wolf.

Soon the animals reached the spot where the object was lying on the ground. To their delight they found that it was a loaf of bread which had obviously been dropped by some other travellers.

'Food,' cried the fox. 'Just what we can do with.'

'Great,' went on the wolf, 'but of course there's only enough for one of us.'

'What do you mean?' replied the fox irritably. 'If there's only enough for one of us – which one?'

'That's easy,' growled the wolf. 'The oldest of the three of us should have the bread and I'd like to point out that that's me.'

'Rubbish,' snapped the fox, 'I'm old enough to be your Dad.'

'Bah, I'd like you to prove that.'

'All right, that shouldn't be too difficult . . .'

For the next five minutes the fox and the wolf argued and insulted each other. Suddenly in the middle of this war of words, they both stopped and looked at the ground nearby. The bread was gone.

'What . . .'

'Who could have . . .?'

Slowly they both turned to look at the camel – just in time to see his jaws finish chewing.

'Ah,' he said. 'I thought you two had lost interest in the bread as you were talking so much. It was good.'

Looking at their tall companion, the fox and the wolf could only growl hungrily at each other before continuing the journey. (Adapted from an Armenian folk tale)

Information for the teacher

1 A useful calendar link for this story is 18th November. In 1307 this was the date on which William Tell supposedly shot the apple from his son's head – truly an action which spoke louder than words.

This story of William Tell is in its own right very good assembly material. Gessler was an Austrian bailiff who ruled harshly over the people of Schwytz, Uri and Unterwald. William Tell, a hunter, refused to bow to Gessler's hat in the market place. He was arrested and ordered by Gessler to shoot an apple from his son's head, or die. The feat was accomplished in the market place.

2 There is a very evocative African proverb which is well suited to the theme of this story:

> A word is like water,
> Once spilled it cannot be gathered again.

Hymn suggestion

Come and Praise Vol 2 'A still, small voice' No 96

Prayer

Let us think this morning about how we speak.
Let us always try to speak kind, thoughtful, helpful, sensible words.
Let us try to avoid speaking words which are thoughtless, cruel, meaningless or untrue.
Let us never make promises we don't keep.
Let us never waste words.
Let us learn the value of listening.
Let us learn to know when actions and not words are needed.

National Curriculum cross-curricular reference

This theme is obviously closely related to English. Words are vital in such activities as responding to and giving instructions, relating real events, conveying ideas effectively.

The idea of effective use of words can be brought across very strongly in these contexts, as can the parallel theme of contrasting actions with the uselessness of 'wasted words'.

43   *The star*

Introduction

Do you sometimes wish you were a bit better at . . . sport . . . maths . . . writing stories . . . playing the recorder . . . lots of things in fact! If so, this morning's story should interest you.

Story

Dee was fed up. No matter what the class did she always seemed to be the worst at it. Her maths always seemed to end up in a muddle, she could mess things up on the computer every time she touched it, and even when she was paint monitor she broke a couple of jars.

Despite this Mrs Jones never lost patience with her and had even put on her report things like . . . 'keeps trying hard . . . is always cheerful'.

'Ah,' thought Dee to herself, 'that's all right but wouldn't it be nice to be good at something?'

In November the Music and Drama Club at Highfield Primary School began rehearsals for its autumn term production. Dee had been in the club for a year. At the last show she had had the job of drawing the curtain – and somehow managed to get it stuck halfway across the stage at the end of the first act, just as the scene shifters came on.

'Dee.'

A voice broke into Dee's daydreams. It was the Thursday when casting was taking place at the Club.

'Yes, miss?'

'Well – will you do it please?' asked Mrs Jones.

'Er . . .'

'Come on, wake up Dee. Louise was supposed to play the policewoman but the family has moved away suddenly. Will you take her part please?'

Dee reached for the paper in a daze, blushing as she did so. She'd never been asked to read a part before.

Slowly the words came into focus on the paper in front of her. She saw that her part wasn't a very big one, but 'Policewoman' did appear about half a dozen times down the page. Already Martin Scott was reading and it was nearly up to her first piece.

As she waited to read, thoughts chased through Dee's head. 'A policewoman wouldn't speak like me,' she thought. 'She would have a firm, loud voice – with an accent a bit different to mine.'

Suddenly it was Dee's turn to read. A voice which she hardly recognised as coming from herself began to say the lines. It was almost as if she *was* the policewoman . . .

The reading went on. As Dee read she saw some of the other children looking at her with odd expressions on their faces. When she had a funny bit to read they laughed as if it was the world's greatest joke. Finally the reading was finished. There was a long silence.

'Well,' said Mrs Jones at last, 'that was well read. And Dee – we'd no idea you were such a star. You'll bring the house down with a performance like that on the night – very well done!'

Dee could feel herself blushing but at the same time it seemed to be just about the very best moment in her whole life.

Information for the teacher

1 Teachers might like to compare this homespun story with the real-life experiences of the actress Susan Hampshire, who has achieved success despite the fact that she is dyslexic.

2 Many schools start productions for Christmas in November and often unexpected talents are revealed in the process. Local knowledge could aid discussion and reflection here.

3 'Theatrical' anniversaries in November which might be used as linking material could include: Jerome Kern (died 11th November 1945); the BBC began daily broadcasting in this month in 1922; Clark Gable died (16th November 1960); Mickey Mouse first appeared on 18th November 1928; 18th November 1836 was the birthday of W.S. Gilbert of Gilbert and Sullivan fame; the world's longest running play (*The Mousetrap*) began its London run on 25th November 1952.

4 Another relevant link with November is the fact that Miss Allen and Miss Harburn became the first policewomen in England on 27th November 1914.

Hymn suggestion

Come and Praise Vol 1 'Lord of the Dance' No 22

Prayer

In our prayers this morning let us think about some words of others:
'All that we are is the result of our thoughts.' (Buddha)
'May we get happiness from life and pass it on to other folk.' (Anon.)
'Let us be thankful for those people who entertain us and make us
laugh.'

National Curriculum cross-curricular reference

This story could be very strongly linked with English (Attainment
Target 1): 'Compose a story together, assume a role in play activity,
talk about the characters'.

44 How can I help?

Introduction

Sometimes we meet people who seem to be good at everything. They
often make us feel that it would be impossible for us ever to do
anything which would help them in any way. This morning's story,
however, might make us think a little bit more about this.

Story

Jamie and Michael were friends. They lived next door to each other
and spent all their spare time together. Jamie was small and an
accident as a baby had left him with a limp. He didn't see very well
either and wore thick spectacles.

Michael, on the other hand, was not only good at work in school,
but he was also a star footballer, swimmer and runner too. He never
ever showed off and the two boys got on very well together . . . but
Jamie had secret thoughts.

'If only I could be just a little bit better than Michael at *something*.

He must think I could never be any good if he got into any kind of trouble.'

One weekend Mr and Mrs Oakwood, Jamie's parents, were loaned a cottage by the sea. Because it was November nobody else wanted it and the Oakwoods thought it would be fun to get out of town.

'I'll tell you what,' said Mr Oakwood, 'if his Mum and Dad agree, you can bring Michael along.'

'That's great!' piped Jamie, with a big grin on his face.

They all got to the cottage on Friday night and after lighting the fire they had a smashing meal of hamburgers. On Saturday they did some walking and some fishing from the little pier, and the boys searched the sands for mystery finds.

On Sunday morning Michael asked if he could go to the paper shop in the village nearby to buy a small present for his mother. Jamie would normally have gone with him but all the exercise on Saturday had made his bad leg ache.

'Stay here,' said Michael, 'and we'll do something together when I get back. It'll only take me about an hour to get there and back.'

Michael went off and after about three-quarters of an hour a sudden change came over the weather. The air turned very damp and a thick mist rolled in from the sea. Soon it was impossible to see more than three or four paces from the front door.

'Oh dear,' said Mrs Oakwood, knowing how isolated the cottage was. 'I'm so worried about Michael. He'll never be able to find his way back.'

'Well,' said Jamie, looking at his watch, 'he must be on his way home now.'

'But you can't see a thing,' said his mother.

Jamie thought for a moment.

'I know,' he said, 'our secret cry.'

'What?' asked his mother, looking puzzled as well as worried now.

'We have a secret cry that only the two of us know,' went on Michael. 'If I go to the gate and keep shouting our secret signal he'll know it's me and he'll head for the sound.'

Putting on a thick coat Jamie took up position.

'Coooo . . . aaaa . . . oooooo.'

There was silence at first, then suddenly, from far off came an answering cry.

'Coooo . . . aaaa . . . oooooo.'

For what seemed a long time Jamie kept calling out – regularly and slowly. From time to time Michael replied and each time his voice seemed to be nearer and less nervous.

Finally there was a clatter as he arrived at the front gate. Coming up the path he flung his arms round Jamie.

'Thanks, Jamie, that was great. I was dead scared out there and then I heard our secret cry. I knew you'd guide me home after that.'

Information for the teacher

1 This is one of those stories which can be kept up a presenter's sleeve until conditions are appropriate for its use. As November is traditionally the season of 'mists and mellow fruitfulness' a suitable opportunity is likely during this long, dark month.

2 There are two parallel themes in this story: friendship and following a sign. Both could be related to religious events. The story of David and Jonathan (Samuel 1, 1–42) provides useful material for discussions on friendship.

The leaving of drawings of a fish to show that there were durable Christians surviving the early days of persecution is an example of the help and inspiration of a sign.

3 Another useful link is with the Jewish Shema. This prayer is traditionally kept by many Jewish families in a mezuzah, a small box attached to the main doorpost of the house.

The link with this assembly is that the Hebrew word '*Shema*' actually means '*Hear*', and this in turn is the first word of the Shema: 'Hear, O Israel, The Lord our God is one Lord.' (Deuteronomy 6, 4)

Hymn suggestion

Come and Praise Vol 2 'A still small voice' No 96

Prayer

Let us learn to listen; to value advice and guidance.
Let us learn to listen to those who are much wiser than we are.
Let us learn to listen; in order that we might learn.

National Curriculum cross-curricular reference

Science is a very obvious link here, with AT4, Level 1c coming particularly to mind: 'Know about the simple properties of sound and light'. The formation of fog is also another possible Science topic.

The evocative nature of sounds in the fog is also useful for stimulating a variety of English activities, from discussion to creative writing.

45   Cold and alone

Introduction

Some days during November are very cold. Fortunately, because we have warm houses and good food, we can often enjoy cold days. But what if it was much colder . . . and we were alone . . . without food . . . and lost . . .

Story

Richard Byrd had a job to do. He was alone in a one man meteorological station in the Antarctic. Here, amidst the bitter, freezing wastes near the South Pole, he had to study and report on weather conditions.

With everything going well this would have been a terribly lonely and difficult task, but right from the start there was a serious problem. It was vital to keep warm, but from first lighting it, Richard found that the stove he had brought with him had leaking joints. This meant that when it was alight deadly fumes seeped out into any enclosed space.

'I've got a problem here,' Richard said to himself. 'If I stay in here with the stove on I'll poison myself; if I put the stove out I'll die of cold, and I've got no materials to mend the stove.'

Although it was possible for a rescue party to reach him this would take several days. He came to a decision.

'I'll stick it out,' he thought. 'I'll leave the stove on but every night I'll open the door of this little shack and I'll take a walk to clear my head.'

So began a nightmare existence. As the days went on Richard felt the effects of the fumes more severely. Every night he was forced to walk outside in the bitter weather. Here, in howling gales and impenetrable darkness, he staggered round in deep snow trying to clear his head. So easy was it to get lost within seconds in the swirling snow, that Richard had to stick bamboo poles with flags on them into the snow every few yards. In this way he could always retrace his footsteps back to the safety of his camp.

For weeks Richard kept up his work under these awful circumstances, but gradually the radio operators back at base camp realised from his radio messages that something was wrong. As a result of this a rescue party was sent out to relieve him.

Information for the teacher

1 The November link is that it was in the winter of 1934 that Admiral Richard Byrd undertook his meteorological task. He was already famous, having been the first man to fly to the North Pole (in 1926) and to the South Pole. The date of the latter achievement marks another November link because it was on the 28th of this month in 1929 that this flight was made.
2 The theme of this story – when we may be called upon to show courage and determination alone – could be broadened into considering other situations requiring these qualities. These might include: times of serious personal illness; new situations, such as moving to a new home, school, area, country; unexpected responsibilities due to family illness, etc.
3 The difficulties which great religious leaders faced alone is another tangent which may be pursued.

Hymn suggestion

Come and Praise Vol 1 'One more step' No 47

Prayer

Dear God, Please give us the strength to face difficulties and hardships when we are alone. Help us to avoid panic and confusion and to be calm and resourceful. Give us the determination to keep on trying at all times.

National Curriculum cross-curricular reference

Science and weather are two obvious links to this story, and Geography would provide an opportunity to locate and learn more about Antarctica.

Physical Education may be involved in experiments with movements and circulation.

December

46 Giving

Introduction

As we move into December our thoughts turn to Christmas. Christmas is a time for giving and this morning's story is about a man who found doing this very difficult.

Story

Isaac and Jacob sat at a table drinking coffee.

'Fools they were – all of them,' said Isaac once again.

'You mean your ancestors?' replied Jacob.

'That's who I mean – my father, his father before him, and the one before that too. All of them made lots of money and then died before they could spend it! Madness. I'm going to make sure that doesn't happen to me.'

'Really?' smiled Jacob. 'Well here's the waiter with our bill, you can make a start on spending now.'

'Ah,' frowned Isaac, patting his pockets. 'Ah, well I haven't any money with me at the moment. Do you mind?'

Later that night there was a knock at Isaac's door. When he answered it he found a shabby, exhausted-looking man there.

'Excuse me, sir,' said the man. 'I'm afraid things have been going badly for me. I had to leave my job to look after my sick wife. Now she has died and as I couldn't pay the rent I've lost my home as well. Have you any work I can do for you in return for a meal?'

Isaac scowled. His first thought was to send this nuisance away with a good ticking-off . . . but then . . . perhaps he could make something out of this situation.

'I've got plenty of work here. You can work for a year – no wages but one meal a day and you can sleep in the shed at the bottom of the garden.'

'Thank you, sir,' said the stranger, whose name was Saul, 'you won't regret your decision.'

After six months Isaac couldn't believe his luck. Saul was a fantastic worker. Already he'd created a beautiful garden, re-painted the magnificent house, repaired machinery from clocks to carriages.

'I'm richer than ever,' thought Isaac, 'and all this is costing me nothing except one miserable meal a day.'

A short while later Isaac was walking in his garden when he heard voices. On the other side of the hedge Saul was talking to someone. Peeping through the hedge Isaac saw that the other person was a poor thin-looking man.

'Anything would help,' he was saying.

'Well, I'll tell you what,' said Saul. 'My master is very fair, he gives me one meal a day and lets me sleep in a little bed in the shed. Why don't you sleep in my bed for a couple of nights until you are feeling better? I'll sleep on the floor, and you can share my meal with me.'

As Isaac listened to these words he felt an icy chill go through his body.

'I've never given anything away in my life,' he thought. 'I'm getting richer and richer and yet this Saul – who has nothing – is prepared to give his bed and half his measly food to a stranger.'

Isaac suddenly stood up straight and marched round the hedge.

'Let me help,' he said humbly.

After helping Saul and the stranger as much as he could, Isaac spent the rest of his life looking for ways to use his money to help as many people as possible.

Information for the teacher

1 Some useful December anniversaries associated with giving could include: 3rd December 1838, birthdate of Octavia Hill who 'gave' the country the National Trust; 4th December 1865, birthdate of Edith Cavell who gave her life in helping British soldiers to escape in the First World War; 5th December 1901, birthdate of Walt Disney whose work gave children so much pleasure; 6th December, feast day of St Nicholas, model for Santa Claus.
2 This theme could lead on to a consideration of what the school or class might give to the local community at Christmas.

Hymn suggestion

Come and Praise Vol 2 'Give us hope Lord' No 87

Prayer

Dear God, Help us to give as generously as we can, and to remember that we can give of our time and talents as well as material things. Teach us what is really important in this world of ours. Amen.

National Curriculum cross-curricular reference

This linking of the person who has so much with the person who has so little could be followed up in Geography (affluent and Third World areas) and History (improvements in food, health, safety, welfare, etc.).

Science can also be involved in considering what makes a healthy person – food, freedom, leisure, peace of mind, etc.

47   You go first

Introduction

None of us much likes the kind of person who thinks they are cleverer than everybody else. One of the most satisfying things about this morning's story is that somebody in it is finally caught out.

Story

There was once a king who was lazy and foolish. He was easily flattered and he would always listen to advice which he wanted to hear. Now it happened that this king had a chief minister who was cunning and sly.

'Your majesty, rely on me,' he would say. 'I'll never let you down and wherever you go, I'll go too.'

This suited the lazy king because it meant he didn't have to think very much – he could just ask his minister for advice wherever he was.

One night the two men were walking near the palace. In the distance foxes were howling.

'Why are those foxes making such a noise, minister?' asked the king.

'Ah, well,' said the minister, thinking quickly, 'they are probably cold, and they know if someone as great as you hears them he will do something to help.'

'Oh,' replied the king, 'will I? Well . . .'

'Perhaps you will allow me to take some money from the royal treasury to buy the foxes some blankets?' said the crafty minister.

'It's the least we can do,' said the king. 'Please see to it.'

The minister drew the money out of the treasury and kept it all for himself, of course. When the foxes howled again he told the king they were saying thank you.

A week later the two men were out walking again when a boar shot out from a bush and startled the king.

'What was that?' he cried.

'An elephant, your majesty,' replied the minister.

'An elephant?' gasped the king. 'Well it didn't look like an elephant to me. Are you sure?'

'Definitely, your majesty,' said the crafty minister. 'You see it is so small because the man in charge of your elephants is lazy and doesn't do his job properly.'

'Disgraceful,' said the king. 'Have him dismissed at once – and take some money from the royal treasury so that the royal elephants are better cared for.'

So the minister got richer.

A week later the two men were out walking again. The same boar was disturbed and dashed out again.

'What . . .' cried the king, 'that elephant, look it's no bigger than it was before, but . . .'

'No, no, your majesty, that isn't an elephant, it's a mouse,' said the minister.

'A mouse?'

'Certainly – it just shows you how careless the royal cook is when mice from the kitchen grow as big as that.'

'Indeed!' cried the king. 'Have the man hanged.'

That night the minister went to see the royal cook and told him that he would be hanged unless . . . The cook got the idea and promised to pay the minister a lot of money if he would save him. The two of them made a plan.

Soon the day set for the hanging arrived. Everybody gathered in the courtyard to see it take place. Then just as the hangman was preparing the noose the minister rushed up to the king.

'Your majesty, your majesty – I've just found out that anybody hanged at this time will be forgiven everything they have done wrong and go straight to live in splendour with the gods. This man shouldn't get away with that.'

'Agreed, agreed,' said the king, 'but . . . but if anyone who is hanged now goes straight to live in splendour with the gods, why don't you and I go?'

'But . . . but . . .' began the minister, for once at a loss for words at this unexpected turn of events.

'And you, my friend,' went on the king, 'have given me such good advice that I insist you go first. Hangman, see to it.'

Now you can imagine how popular the minister was at court! Within seconds he was seized and hanged before he could say anything else. Then the people told the king the truth about his minister and from that day on he became a much more sensible and caring ruler.

Information for the teacher

1 The teacher might reflect with the children on the ability of some people to tell wonderful stories. There are some notable anniversaries in December to provide an historical link to this theme: Robert Louis Stevenson died on 5th December 1894; Wilhelm Grimm (of the Grimm brothers) died on 16th December 1859; Emily Brontë died on 19th December 1848; Beatrix Potter died on 22nd December 1943 and Rudyard Kipling was born on 30th December 1865.

2 All the major religions use stories to make significant points, and those people who are self-seeking at the expense of others are regularly castigated. Examples from the Bible include: The prodigal son (Luke 10, 30–36); the king and the governor (Matthew 18, 23–24); the rich man and Lazarus (Matthew 22, 11–13).

Hymn suggestion

Come and Praise Vol 1 'A man for all the people' No 27

Prayer

Dear God, Teach us to use our intelligence for the good, and not the harm, of other people. Teach us the value of unselfishness. Make us worthy of your teaching. Amen.

National Curriculum cross-curricular reference

This type of story, which relies so much on its 'clever' ending, is a useful starting point for imaginative, creative work in English, whether spoken or written.

48 STOP!

Introduction

When you think about it – *STOP* – is a very important word. If somebody shouts it to a group of people, they pay attention and immediately wonder what has happened. It is a word which is important in this morning's story.

Story

The Buddha was a great religious teacher. He lived in India about two thousand five hundred years ago and taught that it is very important to care for each other.

Once the Buddha was visiting a city called Savatthi. He found the people there very worried.

'It's awful,' one of them said. 'There's the most terrible bandit lurking outside the city.'

'Nobody dares go out alone,' said another resident. 'He lies in wait and robs people regularly.'

'We can't catch him and he's got everybody terrified.'

'Hmm,' said the Buddha. 'I'll have to see what I can do to help.'

'You must be careful, Lord, he's very dangerous.'

So the Buddha left the city and walked slowly out into the countryside. It was hot and dusty and the sun shone down fiercely on the rough country track.

Unknown to the Buddha the bandit had watched him leave the city and then hurried to the spot where he regularly ambushed his victims. He gripped the huge sword he used to terrorise them firmly in his right hand. He waited until the Buddha reached the clump of trees behind which he was hiding, and then leapt out into the road.

'Hand over your money or . . .'

The bandit shouted out his threat, but the Buddha must have been walking faster than he thought because he was already past the clump and walking on down the road.

The bandit turned angrily and, with a shout, began chasing his victim. But strange things started happening.

No matter how loud the bandit shouted, the Buddha paid no attention. Even stranger was the fact that the Buddha just seemed to be strolling along whilst the bandit was running flat out – but just couldn't catch up.

Finally, gasping with exhaustion and frustration, the bandit let out one more yell.

'*Stop!* Hey you, just *stop* will you!'

At once the Buddha turned and said, 'I have stopped, will you?'

'What? What do you mean?' gasped the bandit.

'I've heard of your thieving and cruelty and the way you are making other people's lives miserable. Don't you think you should stop doing that?'

For a moment the bandit looked dazed and worried. Then, unnerved by the strange events which had taken place, and suddenly sorry for all the dreadful things he had done, he dropped to his knees in front of the Buddha.

'You're right,' he cried. 'I've behaved dreadfully. How can I show how sorry I am?'

'Well,' said the Buddha, laying his hand on the bandit's head, 'you can become a follower of mine, and you can go back to Savatthi and return all the things you have stolen. Then people will realise you are a changed man and want to live an honest and caring life.'

Information for the teacher

1 A simple and effective way to introduce this story might be to have three pieces of card with the words: *STOP*, *LOOK* and *LISTEN* printed on them.

2 The link between this assembly and December stems from the fact that Bodhi Day is celebrated by Buddhists in this month each year. It commemorates the occasion when Prince Gautama discovered enlightenment sitting under a Bodhi tree and became the Buddha.

   One form the celebrations assume is the placing of flowers in Buddhist temples as offerings to, and thanksgiving for, the Buddha.

Hymn suggestion

Come and Praise Vol 2 'Lead us from death to life' No 140

Prayer

Let us listen to some words from the Buddha, and then spend some time thinking about them. The words are:

'All that we are is the result of our thoughts'.

National Curriculum cross-curricular reference

The story of this assembly lends itself to a number of artistic activities. Some illustrations in the rather stylised Indian fashion might be attempted. The story is also a very good vehicle for drama.

Bearing in mind the National Curriculum suggestion for 'musical composition' it also offers possibilities for simple improvised percussion in the sort of increased tempo characterised in a piece such as 'The Sorcerer's Apprentice'.

49   This month

Introduction

Most of us look forward to December as a very exciting time. Many writers of the past, however, thought that being out of doors at this time of the year was miserable:

> The melancholy days are come,
> The saddest of the year.

But is December such a dreary time? Not if we look very carefully at what is going on in the countryside.

This month

Although carols suggest that December is in 'the bleak mid-winter', the weather in Britain is often at its most severe after Christmas.

There is quite a bit of interesting bird activity this month. You should watch out for yellow hammers, which bring a lovely touch of colour to bare hedges. They tend to fly round in groups, as do bramblings and chaffinches. Fieldfares and redwings, who are members of the thrush family, are likely to be seen in the open country and ploughland. Lapwings can be seen too and once you have learned to spot their peculiar wheeling flight they are easy to recognise. Friendly robins are around as well.

People in the northern part of the country have a better chance of spotting stoats at this time of the year. This animal changes its colour to a winter white, although you can still see black hairs in the tip of its tail. Having a white coat when there is snow around has two advantages for the stoat: it protects it from its bigger enemies and helps it to stalk its own prey without being seen easily.

There are still a few flowers about in December too. The common gorse, with its bright yellow blooms, is very welcome; and sometimes chickweed and shepherd's purse blossom too.

Insects are very few and far between but sometimes queen bees can be seen around homes they have made in things like disused field mouse holes. If you live somewhere where you see foxes regularly, then December will be much the same as the other months – foxes don't seem to mind what the weather is like.

It is possible that hazel catkins will appear, but cones are the best woodland finds in December. Evergreens with cones include fir, spruce, Scots pine, larch and cedar. Mistletoe can usually be seen too – often perched high up on trees. It is spread by birds eating its berries and then wiping them off their beaks on to the branches of other trees. Holly trees have been around for a very long time and some of those you look at on a cold December day may be three hundred years old.

If there is snow around then it is a marvellous time of the year to look for footprints. When you spot some you could ask yourself some questions:

Do they belong to a bird or an animal?

Can we tell in which direction they are moving?

Why might they be where they are?

To help answer these, look to see if the footprints show paws or hooves. If they belong to a bird they usually show three toes pointing forwards and one pointing backwards.

Animals whose footprints you might see could include badgers, stoats, foxes, rabbits, field mice, rats and squirrels. Look out, of course, for bigger creatures like dogs, sheep and horses.

So if you know what to look for, and are wearing a warm coat, December can be a very interesting month to be out and about.

Information for the teacher

1 Sometimes, amidst the possible over-excitement of indoor Christmas in the primary school, it is a good idea to take children out to appreciate 'God's world' this month. This assembly could be a forerunner to such an activity. Visual aids and some stimulating books around the classroom help too, for example, Collins' *Guide to Animal Tracks and Signs*.

2 This is a good month to stress the necessity of being aware of animals' needs, both pets and creatures in the wild.

3 Linked to reflection on the beauty of the December countryside

comes some comment on the shortage of daylight. December sees sunrise at approximately 7.40am and sunset before 4pm. Throughout the month sunrise is one minute later and sunset one minute earlier until the winter solstice on 21st December.

4 Finally an anecdote on the 'appreciation and taking-for-granted' theme. An Australian boy on holiday in England in December was so thrilled at seeing snow he rushed outside and put some in an envelope to send home to his parents!

5 Bearing in mind the Ramblers' Association's aim to 'foster a greater knowledge, love and care of the countryside', here is a useful address: The Ramblers' Association, 1/5 Wandsworth Road, London SW8 2LJ.

Hymn suggestion

Come and Praise Vol 2 'When the winter day is dying' No 118

Prayer

Dear God, Help us to look carefully for beauty and to treasure it. Teach us to value the natural things around us and make us aware of the needs of all animals and birds. Amen.

National Curriculum cross-curricular reference

Science work in the contexts of 'cold', 'light', 'weather' is appropriate here, as are the more environmental studies aspects of 'animals and birds in winter'. Making recordings of temperatures and weather conditions would be useful.

Art is well suited by studies of winter sunsets, the tracery of bare trees, etc.

Winter scenes are also evocative in a creative writing context, and often produce interesting poems and prose from children.

50 Tough?

Introduction

The 10th December is a day which was specially set aside to think about caring for each other, and trying to make sure everyone has a fair life.

In times past this was often very difficult. This morning's assembly is about events which took place about five hundred years before Jesus was born.

Story

Aristotle was unhappy and worried. Life in Athens had been wonderful. It was a beautiful city, he had lived with his mother and father . . . and then had come the terrible day of the accident. Now he was in Sparta, an orphan, living with his uncle.

Sparta was so different. Here, to be tough meant everything, and today he had heard about this great festival of toughness from the boys who lived nearby.

'It's great, you'll see.'

'How do you mean?'

'Well, it's a battle.'

'Will . . . will . . . I be in it?'

' 'Course not. You're too young and too small. It's for the bigger boys.'

'But what happens?'

'Well you know that field which is surrounded by the river – two armies of boys meet there to see who wins the fight.'

'Do they have spears and swords?'

'No, nothing like that. All the fighting is done with bare hands.'

Aristotle shuddered and yet at the same time felt a strange excitement. The other boys could talk of nothing else and were obviously looking forward to the great fight.

The day of the battle finally arrived. The whole city had a carnival atmosphere. Men, women and children made their way to the field by the river in order to get good viewing positions. Food sellers shouted cheerfully to advertise what they were selling and everyone seemed in a good mood.

Suddenly a cry went up.

'Here's the first lot.'

A team of some of Sparta's biggest and strongest boys came marching through the crowd. They crossed the bridge into the field and, lifting their arms, gave a great shout that was half battle-cry and half challenge.

The shout was answered by the second team of boys who were now marching through the crowds towards the bridge. Soon they were across it too, and facing their opponents.

A hush fell over the watchers and Aristotle could feel the

excitement and anticipation all around him. Suddenly, with a gigantic roar, the two sets of boys charged at each other.

Aristotle saw blows and punches rained on heads and bodies. Boys took terrible blows and fell to the ground beneath charging feet. Screams of pain mixed with the frantic cheering of the crowd.

Information for the teacher

1 This story could end on a questioning note of concern and could then be used to promote reflections about Human Rights Day, which is on the 10th December. This day was established by the United Nations General Assembly, and it is also the day when prizes are announced for those whose achievements have enhanced human rights and benefited mankind. These are the Nobel prizes. They originate from the fortune of Alfred Nobel who died on 10th December, 1896. He was an industrialist and invented dynamite.

Hymn suggestion

Come and Praise Vol 2 'Sad, puzzled eyes' No 74

Prayer

> Lord, help us to work for peace.
> Where there is hatred, let us show love;
> Where there is injury, pardon;
> Where there is discord, union;
> Where there is doubt, faith;
> Where there is darkness, light;
> Where there is sadness, joy;
> Where there is despair, hope;
> For you and for everyone. Amen. (Prayer of St Francis)

National Curriculum cross-curricular reference

History is the most obvious link here, but the Spartans' concern for physical prowess could also incorporate different aspects of both Physical Education and Science.

This story is also one which produces strong reactions in upper juniors and can lead on to evocative writing and discussion on such things as cruelty, conforming, 'dares', having one's own opinions, etc.

51   *Justice is done*

Introduction

This morning's story is about a cruel king who thought he was much cleverer than anybody else. But was he?

Story

Azab was a king – and a cruel and cunning one. He had a prisoner in the dark and dirty cells beneath his palace. This was a young man called Rachid.

Rachid had come to Azab to ask for greater justice for the people; for an equal share of money for the crops; for less severe taxes. Azab's answer had been to throw Rachid into prison – but he was worried.

'That Rachid means trouble,' thought Azab. 'If I let him go he'll stir the people up; if I keep him in prison there might be even more trouble. I must think of a plan to sort him out.'

For over a week the cunning king thought and plotted, and then he came up with a brilliant idea. After another week he was ready to put it into practice.

In the great courtyard a group of people gathered together. There was Azab, his ministers and a squad of his best soldiers. Opposite them was a group of important local leaders, all friends and allies of Rachid. Between the two groups stood a table and on the table was a box.

When everybody was in place, Azab clapped his hands and two soldiers appeared, marching a still-chained Rachid between them. Kicking up spurts of dust with their feet, they reached the table and stopped in front of it.

'Now, my friends,' said Azab, looking at the group of his enemies. There was a mumble of annoyance and disagreement from them. 'I'm going to show you what a fair person I am,' went on the king. 'You see this box here . . .'

At this everybody followed the king's pointing finger with their eyes, and stared at the box.

'It's got two small balls inside it. One of them says *Innocent* on it; one of them says *Guilty*. Now this man Rachid here is imprisoned for plotting against me, but I'm going to give him a chance.

He is going to be blindfolded. Then he must put his hand in the box and pull out a ball. If it says *Innocent*, he and every other prisoner in my cells can go free today.

If, however, it says *Guilty* then he and every other prisoner will have their sentences doubled.'

As Rachid listened to the king's words he realised how sly and cunning his opponent was. He was absolutely certain that both balls had *Guilty* on them, but he would only be allowed to look at the one he chose. That meant that not only would his prison sentence be doubled, but so would that of every other prisoner. Then, they and their friends would start hating him and forget the evil ways of Azab. He looked at the king's smirking face and knew he was right.

'The blindfold,' ordered Azab, and the soldiers immediately bound a cloth tightly round Rachid's head. He then felt his hand pushed into the box and his fingers closed round one of the balls.

Then, before anybody could stop him, Rachid crammed the ball into his mouth and swallowed it. Tearing off his blindfold he shouted out so that everybody could hear.

'I have chosen my ball and swallowed it – the ball that is left will therefore show what my choice was.'

Before he could be stopped one of the guards picked up the other ball and called out: 'It says *Guilty* on here.'

At once there was a tremendous cheer from the people gathered in the courtyard. Azab's face was like thunder. He had been caught out by his own trick.

Information for the teacher

1 A useful anniversary link here is with 12th December. This was the date on which Robert Browning died in 1889. His 'Pied Piper' can be allied to this story in that both carry the same message of a promise being made which is never meant to be kept. Retribution follows as a result.

2 When this story is being told to the children it is interesting to leave out the ending initially and ask them if they can see a way out of Rachid's dilemma. Another story where the same ploy can be adopted is when Solomon is asked to decide which of the two arguing women is the real mother of the baby. (1 Kings 3, 16–28)

Hymn suggestion

Come and Praise Vol 1 'The wise may bring their learning' No 64

Prayer

Let us think this morning of fairness. How often we say, 'It's not fair,' when we are disappointed, don't get what we want, are not chosen for something when we think we should be.

Let us remember that there are many people in the world for whom life must seem really unfair.

Let us think this morning of fairness.

National Curriculum cross-curricular reference

This story is an ideal vehicle for drama; linked to this there is discussion potential in English. It is the sort of material which provides 'motivation for the learner to make sense of and acquire control over language and the power which it can have'.

52   The Tom Eadie Story

Introduction

You could probably all write quite a bit about the subject 'A good friend'. There is an old saying: 'A friend in need is a friend indeed.' This morning's story shows exactly what this means.

Story

It was 17th December 1927 and the bitter winter wind lashed the white-topped waves into a frenzy. Ploughing through the swirling, icy sea off the east coast of America, the USS 'Falcon' battled to reach its destination.

This was the spot where a submarine had sunk. The 'Falcon' was to send down divers to see if there were any survivors.

'This is the worst diving weather I've ever seen,' said Tom Eadie, one of the two experienced deep sea divers on board.

'I couldn't agree more,' replied Fred Michels, his long-time partner. 'The pressure will be terrible down there.'

'Well, we've got to do it,' went on Tom. 'We've got to find out if anybody's alive in that sub.'

Some hours later Tom was over the side of the 'Falcon' and descending rapidly under the weight of his heavy diving suit. Currents pulled him savagely from side to side and it was difficult for him to see through the wave-swept mud.

By good navigation, however, the 'Falcon' had arrived in an excellent position. Despite the difficulties Tom saw the sunken submarine directly beneath him. Within minutes he was able to tap the conning tower and other parts of the craft. There were no answering taps as Tom went over every part of the submarine again and again.

'It doesn't seem hopeful,' he radioed to the surface.

'OK,' came the reply. 'Come up for a break. Fred will relieve you.'

Minutes later Tom was back aboard the 'Falcon' trying to get some warmth into his freezing limbs. He had hardly even begun to warm up when an urgent message flashed up from Fred: 'Cutters needed – cutters needed.'

In an instant Tom realised what had happened. His friend had got tangled up in the submarine's wreckage. Unless help could be got to him quickly, he had no hope of survival. Without even waiting to get his three pairs of warm underwear on Tom got back into his diving suit and, equipped with wire cutters, was soon plunging into the depths again.

When he reached Fred he found things worse than he expected. Hopelessly entangled in a mass of equipment the trapped diver was already unconscious and icy water had leaked into the body of his cut suit.

'Send down a hacksaw – quickly.' Tom flashed a message to the surface.

He had realised that the cutters were useless. As soon as the hacksaw was lowered to him Tom began to cut through the bent piece of iron which had his friend most securely held. Having forgotten his gloves in the rush, and with his own suit torn and leaking and his ears and hands aching unbearably, Tom sawed carefully in the freezing gloom.

Ten minutes . . . twenty . . . thirty . . . forty . . .

'There's no hope now,' muttered one of the anxious crew on the deck above. 'It's been too long.'

Just then there came another telephone message from below. 'Get me up!'

Down below Tom had finally sawn through the iron bar and, released from its grip, the unconscious Fred in his buoyant suit drifted up to the surface.

Unable to see where Fred had gone Tom was hauled up. Once

back on board the 'Falcon' he was rushed to the decompression chamber where attendants began work on his freezing and battered body.

'I just lost him,' mumbled Tom. 'One minute he was there – the next he was gone.'

Just at that moment the still-unconscious and stiff body of Fred was passed into the chamber. He had been spotted floating on the surface and quickly rescued.

Both men made a full recovery, and for his courage and determination in rescuing his friend Tom Eadie was awarded the United States Congressional Medal of Honour.

Information for the teacher

1 This Atlantic adventure was necessitated by a collision between the US destroyer 'Paulding' and Submarine 'S4'. The latter sank immediately on impact. The submarine was raised three months later but there were no survivors.
2 The subject of courage at sea offers many follow-up possibilities. Useful addresses in this context are:
   Royal National Lifeboat Institution, West Quay Road, Poole, Dorset B15 1HZ
   Royal Life Saving Society, 14 Devonshire St., London W1N 2AT
   Mission to Seamen, St Michael Paternoster Road, College Hill, London EC4R 2RL
   Navy Records Society, c/o Royal Naval College, Greenwich, London SE10 9NN

Hymn suggestion

Come and Praise Vol 1 'He who would valiant be' No 44

Prayer

Let us pray this morning for those who earn their living on or under the sea. Keep them safe from accidents and storms. Let us give thanks for modern inventions which make their difficult work easier.

National Curriculum cross-curricular reference

The sea is a subject which offers great and varied scope in Science, History and Geography. Working underwater offers further opportunities in Science and CDT. Some controlled classroom experiments could be linked with this.

'Self sacrifice' is a theme with very wide-reaching Religious Education concerns.

53   *The organist*

Introduction

Sometimes in life we experience something so good that we never ever forget it. Let's imagine this morning that we are not in a school but in a village church. It is getting near Christmas and the organist is in the church by himself – practising hard for all the playing he will shortly have to do.

Story

John sat at the organ. The church was empty and still. For the twentieth time his fingers attempted to play the difficult piece in front of him – and for the twentieth time he made half a dozen mistakes as he played.

'Ohh,' he groaned to himself. 'I know I'm not really a very good organist, but this is such a lovely piece, I wish I could play it better.'

He sighed and looked again at the music. The composer's name stood out clearly on the sheet in front of him – Felix Mendelssohn.

'Well . . . must try again . . .'

Then John was suddenly aware that somebody was standing at the back of the church. He felt annoyed.

'Just what I don't want,' he muttered. He started to play again, but became more annoyed when he saw the visitor walking slowly up the aisle towards him.

John took his hands off the keyboard just as the stranger spoke.

'Excuse me,' said the man, 'I was passing by and I heard you playing that piece on the organ. Would you mind if I had a try at playing it?'

John could hardly believe his ears. Of all the cheek!

'Not a chance, I'm afraid. I'm the organist here and I'm afraid we can't let just anybody who fancies it play on this valuable instrument. Besides, it's a very difficult piece.'

'Oh,' replied the stranger and to John's annoyance he sat down in one of the front seats.

John started playing again. He tried to ignore the quiet man sitting there and concentrate on the music. Gradually he laboured through the piece.

'Excuse me.'

It was the stranger again.

'Yes?'

'I really wouldn't hurt the organ if I played it. I have got some experience.'

John sighed with exasperation.

'Perhaps if I let him have a go he'll clear off and I'll be able to get on with it,' he thought to himself. 'All right,' he said aloud. 'Try for a couple of minutes then.'

John climbed down from the organ seat and busied himself with some piles of music.

'Thank you,' said the stranger, and put his hands on the keyboard. At once music swelled through the church. Its beauty caused John to stop what he was doing just to listen.

As the magnificent playing continued, John gasped with astonishment. The stranger was playing the difficult piece which he had struggled so desperately with – and what's more, he was playing it with his eyes tightly closed!

As suddenly as it had started the wonderful music stopped and the stranger climbed down.

'Thank you,' he said in his quiet voice.

John finally recovered from his shock.

'That was . . . that was . . . it was just wonderful,' he said, 'but . . . but . . . who are you?'

'Oh, my name is Felix Mendelssohn,' said the stranger as he walked away up the aisle.

Information for the teacher

1 Felix Mendelssohn Bartholdy was born in Hamburg in 1809 and died in Leipzig in 1847. Son of a wealthy father, he composed prolifically ('A Midsummer Night's Dream', 'Fingal's Cave', 'Italian Symphony', etc.) and during his travels he visited England. He composed the overture to 'A Midsummer Night's Dream' when he was only seventeen.

2 The idea of travelling musicians is a very old one. The 'minstrels' of Hebrew times (II Kings 3, 15) were also metal workers who travelled round from community to community both playing and repairing things.

Throughout Biblical history musicians were highly honoured –

they were found in prestigious places near kings and priests and were often spared execution when savage changes of power took place.

Hymn suggestion

Come and Praise Vol 2 'Sing, people sing' No 110

Prayer

Let us think this morning about the pleasure which music gives to so many people. Let us give thanks for talented musicians whose skills and compositions we can enjoy. Let us also give thanks for those technicians whose skills make it possible for us to listen to music on discs and tapes.

National Curriculum cross-curricular reference

Music is the obvious category here. The opportunity to listen to some short and carefully-chosen passages from Mendelssohn's work should be taken. Some organ music could also be presented.

There is also potential for some individual and group composition with percussion instruments.

Both History and Geography can be involved in making an investigation into great composers.

54 *What's in a carol?*

Introduction

One of the most famous carols sung at Christmas is 'Good King Wenceslas'. Let me remind you of some of the words:

> 'Good King Wenceslas looked out
> On the feast of Stephen,
> Where the snow lay round about
> Deep and crisp and even.
> Brightly shone the moon that night,
> Though the frost was cruel,
> When a poor man came in sight
> Gathering winter fuel.'

Who was Wenceslas? How did the carol come about?

Story

The story of Wenceslas is really one which centres round three main characters. These were: Wenceslas, a young prince who became King of Bohemia in 921; Boleslav, his brother, who wanted to rule the country instead of Wenceslas; Henry I, ruler of the Germans who wanted to invade Bohemia and make it part of his empire.

Wenceslas, before becoming king, had spent most of his life in a monastery. He was gentle and kind and firmly believed that all people should be treated with goodwill. As soon as he became king he began to put his ideas into practice. Calling his ministers together he gave them some orders.

'Those gallows which stand in so many public places – take them down. We don't want to remind people of bad things. Let's be encouraging. The same goes for the dungeons – there will be no more torture down there, no matter what the crime.'

Such moves made Wenceslas very popular with his subjects. Gradually they became less fearful.

'Wenceslas is young but he's got the right ideas.'

'He means what he says.'

'Yes . . . if only we could all live in peace . . .'

'. . . And stop worrying about armies and wars.'

But Boleslav thought his brother was wrong. 'It's no good being soft like this. The Germans are just waiting to invade us. We've got to be tough on our people, make them ready to fight and die if necessary.'

In 928 Henry I and the Germans invaded Bohemia. In a very short time they were at the gates of Prague. Wenceslas stayed calm and once again called his ministers to him.

'If we fight, thousands of people will be killed or injured and we will probably still lose. Let's try the peaceful approach. I will go to the city gates and welcome Henry myself.'

Was Wenceslas right? Boleslav and his followers didn't think so, because just a year later they murdered Wenceslas. The Czech people had different ideas though. They remembered Wenceslas for his concern for others, his kindness and his many Christian acts. That is why St Wenceslas is one of the most famous saints in Czechoslovakia.

But what about the carol? Well, the tune is a very old one which dates back to about 1250. The words which we sing were put to this tune by a man called John Neale in the nineteenth century. He probably didn't know any more about Wenceslas than we do, but his work helps us all to remember a Christian who lived in very difficult times.

Information for the teacher

1 In Wenceslas Square in Prague the statue of the King-Saint carries an epitaph beneath it: 'St Wenceslas suffer not us nor our children to perish'.
2 If the carol aspect of this story is enlarged then the story of another carol always interests children. This is of course 'Silent Night'.

   In 1818, in the village of Obendorf in Austria, the priest Joseph Mohr discovered just before Christmas that mice had damaged the bellows of the church organ. Anxious to divert the congregation's attention away from this lack of musical accompaniment, Mohr and the organist Franz Gruber composed a new carol for the Christmas service. With Gruber accompanying the singing on a guitar, 'Silent Night' had its first public performance at the village Christmas service.

   This story has marvellous dramatic possibilities.

Hymn suggestion

The obvious choice here is the carol which is central to this morning's theme.

Prayer

Dear God, Let us think this morning about decisions. As we get older we have more and more difficult decisions to make. Give us the strength and wisdom to choose wisely when we are in these situations. Amen.

National Curriculum cross-curricular reference

History and Geography would be involved in researching more background detail of time and place. Music and English can feature in children's attempts to set their own words to well-known tunes. This exercise often produces surprisingly good results.

55 *Julianne's story*

Introduction

Christmas is a time of journeys. Mary and Joseph had to make a long journey before Jesus was born. Today lots of people travel by car, train, ship and aeroplane to be with families and friends at Christmas.

This morning's story is about a journey that didn't work out as it should have done.

Story

Julianne was excited. What would her father buy her for Christmas?

'I'm sure it will be something to do with animals,' she thought to herself. Her father was a zoologist and seemed to know everything about animals.

'Anyway, I'll find out soon,' she thought, as the announcement to board the plane came over the loud speakers. Julianne was making the four hundred and seventy-five mile trip from Lima to Pucallpa in Peru to be home for Christmas.

A few minutes later, along with ninety-one other passengers, Julianne was fastening her seat belt as the plane prepared for take-off.

'We hope you enjoy your flight,' announced the captain, and after a normal take-off, the plane climbed above the dense jungle.

As Julianne gazed down at the thick carpet of green below she seemed to hear her father's voice giving her a piece of his always wise advice: 'If you ever get lost in the jungle – look for a stream and follow it. That way you're sure to be rescued eventually.'

Julianne's thoughts were interrupted by the captain's voice again. 'Ladies and gentlemen, would you return to your seats and fasten your seat belts please. We have some bad weather ahead and it may get a little bumpy – nothing to worry about.'

As Julianne tightened her seat belt the plane began to lurch sickeningly, lightning flashed past the windows and rain hammered on the fuselage. Suddenly there was a bigger bump than any that had gone before and the plane began to fall.

People started screaming, the luggage racks crashed open and bags fell in every direction. The lights suddenly went out and there was a tremendous roaring noise. Terrified, Julianne gripped the arms of her seat and felt rain beating on her – she was no longer in the plane!

What happened next Julianne never knew because she fainted.

When she woke up she was still strapped in her seat but it was lying on its side. Around her she could feel grass and she could hear frogs croaking. But how could this be? She fell into a deep, exhausted sleep.

When Julianne awoke the next time it was morning. Looking round she saw that she was still strapped in her seat, which was lying on the ground in dense jungle. Quickly she realised what had happened.

'The plane must have crashed – or somehow I fell out. Perhaps there are other people around. I must look.'

A terrible feeling of panic swept over her. She was cut and bruised and when she tried to stand up shooting pains surged through her foot. She broke a branch off a tree to use as a crutch – and then saw a little, gaily-wrapped parcel lying near her. 'It must have come from the plane too,' she muttered. Opening it she found inside some toys, a piece of Christmas cake and some sweets. A large tear ran down her cheek as she looked at the little toys and realised that it was Christmas Day.

Then, shaking her head determinedly, she put the cake and sweets in a pocket of her torn dress and straightened up. Now she must do what her father had always said – 'Find a stream'.

So began a nightmare journey for Julianne. Existing only on the cake and sweets she staggered through the jungle looking for a stream. Savage mosquitoes attacked her constantly; poisonous snakes slithered across her path and beautifully coloured and juicy-looking berries tempted her to taste their poison.

After a few days she found a stream.

'Now I'll be safe,' she thought, falling by the water and gulping refreshing mouthfuls.

But it was not to be. Day after day she fought her way along the stream, terrified of alligators, and getting weaker and weaker. By now one of her eyes wouldn't open, the pain in her injured foot was almost unbearable and she couldn't lift one of her arms. But this brave and determined girl just wouldn't give up – and then she saw it! Moored in a clearing by the stream was a boat, and further into the clearing stood a small hut.

With a hoarse cry Julianne staggered to the hut and pushed open the door. It was empty. Tears of disappointment coursed down her face and she slumped to the floor.

Now, however, her ordeal was nearly over. Within hours a party of Indian hunters found her and soon she was on her way to hospital and safety.

Information for the teacher

1 The girl's name was Julianne Koepcke. She was a passenger on a plane flying over the Peruvian jungle from Lima to Pucallpa in December 1971.

   The plane ran into a violent storm at 10,000 feet and broke up in mid-air. By a miracle Julianne fell to the ground in her seat and survived. Her courage and determination kept her alive in the jungle for ten days, with only the cake and sweets to sustain her. She was seventeen years old at the time.
2 The 'difficult journeys' theme could incorporate that of Mary and Joseph; for Bible reference see Luke, chapter 2.
3 Another theme which may be pursued in relation to Julianne's story is the one of being alone and surviving only by courage, determination and initiative. There are plenty of examples of this – Robinson Crusoe, round-the-world sailors, Polar explorers, etc. Such stories appear regularly in newspapers.

Hymn suggestion

Come and Praise Vol 2 'Give us hope Lord' No 87

Prayer

In our prayers this morning let us think of times when:

   We have to make decisions alone because we face worrying and difficult situations.

   We have to be brave because of illness or things happening which we don't really understand.

   We have to rely only on ourselves.

   Let us pray that we have the courage to face these situations.

National Curriculum cross-curricular reference

Science comes in here – in discussing powered flight, the dangers and effects of bad weather, jungle conditions, etc.

   Geography could be involved in locating the story.

   The story is also one which could provoke considerable discussion and writing in English.

56   An unusual Christmas dinner

Introduction

Let's think about Christmas dinner – what sort of food do we eat at this time of the year? (*Pause for answers!*)

This morning's story tells of one of the strangest Christmas dinners you could imagine. Here's how it came about.

Story

On 21st December 1908 a man wrote the following words in his diary: 'We are very hungry . . . our beards are masses of ice all day long.'

The man was called Ernest Shackleton and he was the leader of a group of men who were trying to be the first explorers to reach the South Pole. Already they had been travelling for two months on their mission and things had been very difficult for them.

'It was hard going up those icy mountains,' called Eric Marshall to his colleagues.

'It wouldn't have been so bad if all the ponies hadn't died. Then we wouldn't have had to pull these sledges ourselves, would we?' answered Frank Wild.

'You're right there,' said Eric. 'They're a terrible weight. Still, we've a treat to look forward to soon.'

'What's that?'

'Christmas dinner – what else?'

In the bitter wind, fingering his cut and frostbitten nose, Ernest Shackleton couldn't resist a smile. Despite the savagery of the weather his men had remained cheerful.

They had had to abandon all but the very bare essentials because they were too exhausted to pull much on the sledges. They had only the clothes they stood up in – and they were still many, many miles from the Pole.

By six o'clock on Christmas Day they had covered only a few more miles. The wind howled relentlessly over the snow and they bent their tired and aching bodies to the task of putting up their little tent.

Once this was done the four men crouched inside in their thick fur clothes. The thoughts of all of them were far away – back home with their families and friends.

'Right,' said Ernest. 'This is what we've been waiting for – anybody hungry?'

There was a great cheer from the three men as Shackleton set the little stove going and prepared to make the feast.

'I've never been so hungry in my whole life,' muttered Lieutenant Adams. 'Never.'

'Never mind, Christmas dinner coming up soon – I can hardly wait,' replied Eric Marshall.

'First course on its way,' called out Ernest, who had been doing the cooking.

Each man grasped his tin plate and looked at the steaming pile which lay upon it.

'Oh, it's hoosh,' said Frank.

'Hoosh' was a ration for the dead ponies which had been boiled up with a strange kind of dried meat called pemmican.

'What's next?'

There was a clinking noise as the next course came round. This was one dried biscuit each. The third course was half a cup of Oxo each, and then came the highlight of the meal.

Through all the difficulties and abandoning of equipment Ernest had held onto a tiny Christmas pudding. Now, he boiled up a little cocoa water and then dropped the Christmas pudding into it. When the water boiled again and steam rose into the tiny tent the leader divided the small pudding with his spoon and carefully laid a piece on each man's plate.

'Merry Christmas,' he said.

'Merry Christmas,' they all replied, thinking they had never tasted anything so wonderful in their whole lives.

Information for the teacher

1 Shackleton's 1908–09 mission to reach the South Pole failed. With food supplies almost completely finished, and suffering from acute stomach pains after having eaten some undercooked rice, the men were totally exhausted by early January. On 7th January they encountered the worst snow storm yet – 'a blinding, shrieking blizzard' wrote Shackleton. They could go no further and began the return journey.

   Despite the expedition's failure, Shackleton was knighted for his bravery when he returned to England.

2 The theme of 'what we enjoy when we are really desperately hungry' is a far-reaching one with lots of thought-provoking possibilities at this time of the year.

3 There is a quotation from the Bible which could be used to provoke

a great deal of thought in the context of this story. It is: 'A man's spirit may sustain him'. (Proverbs 18, 4)

Hymn suggestion

Come and Praise Vol 1 'When a knight won his spurs' No 50

Prayer

Let us think this morning of the courage of explorers, whose discoveries have so increased our knowledge of the world. Let us learn from their self-sacrifice and determination. Let us also appreciate the good food and good fortune which so many of us enjoy.

National Curriculum cross-curricular reference

History and Geography are the obvious links here, and Polar exploration could involve both extensively.

English, in the context of diary writing, would be a useful follow-up; as would Science in considering what people need to survive in extreme conditions of this nature.

57   Christmas around the world

Introduction

People celebrate Christmas all over the world. In different places some things are done very differently, as you will hear.

Christmas around the world

You have probably all written letters asking for special presents for Christmas. If you lived in Germany, however, the letters themselves would be special. When the children have written them they put the letters in envelopes and then spread glue lightly over each envelope. Next they scatter sugar on the glue so that the letters glitter. Then, on Christmas Eve, the glittering letters are put outside on window sills to await collection.

In Poland it is very important to watch for the first star on

Christmas Eve. When it appears the whole family sits down to a Christmas feast. This begins with the passing round of a thin piece of bread which is called an *oplatek*. There is a picture of Mary, Joseph and Jesus on the *oplatek* and each member of the family breaks a piece of it when it reaches them. Usually two empty places are left at the feast table so that if Mary and Joseph were to arrive there would be places for them.

In Finland, where it is very cold in December, children make a point of putting out special feasts for birds and animals at Christmas. Long poles are sometimes stuck in the ground and pieces of suet hung from them. Nuts are strung from trees in long chains.

If you lived in Finland you would look forward to very different food from that which we enjoy in Britain at Christmas. You might sit down to a feast of cold ham and pickled herrings!

In Norway too, animals are thought of at Christmas. Norwegian children remember the story of a little gnome who was supposed to guard animals, and they put out bowls of porridge for him at this time of the year.

Swedish children remember that Jesus lay in a manger of straw, so they make many of their Christmas decorations from straw. In France, when everybody had open fires and not central heating, it was important to keep the fire going all night on Christmas Eve in case Mary should pass by and need warmth and shelter.

Italy is the country with which we associate Christmas cribs. St Francis made one in his home town of Greccio to remind people of where and how Jesus was born. From this beginning Italian families began to make model cribs in their homes and eventually the idea spread around the world.

In far away Australia, Christmas comes in the middle of the summer, when the weather is very hot. People go to famous beaches like Bondi in Sydney to eat their turkey and pudding at picnics. When they go home, though, they still have decorations of Christmas trees and evergreens in their houses.

Information for the teacher

1 Teachers who would like a compendium of Christmas information can consult the book *Christmas is Coming* by Redvers Brandling (Simon & Schuster). Included in this are chapters on Christmas readings, Words for Christmas, Christmas today, Christmas and other cultures.

A beautiful book for teachers to read from, and children to

browse through is the Kingfisher *Christmas Book*, 'a collection of stories, poems and carols for the twelve days of Christmas'.

2 This assembly could well be presented in tableau form, whereby pictures, models and dramatic re-enactments reflect each of the aspects shown, and the whole thing is linked by the words of the passage.

3 Whilst on the international aspect of Christmas, the idea of wishing people 'Merry Christmas' in different languages is always one that appeals to Junior School children. Thus the following might be useful:

Czechoslovakian	*Vesele Vanoch*
Dutch	*Gelukkig Kerstfeest*
Finnish	*Hauskaa Joulua*
French	*Joyeux Noël*
German	*Fröhliche Weinachten*
Italian	*Buone Feste Natalizie*
Norwegian	*Gledig Jul*
Polish	*Bozego Narodzenia*
Spanish	*Feliz Navidad*
Swedish	*Glad Jul*

Hymn suggestion

Come and Praise Vol 2 'As I went riding by' No 120

Prayer

When we think of our own Christmas we so often think of warmth, family gatherings, kindness – all those things which make this time so special. Let us listen now to some words about that first Christmas:

Winds through the olive trees
Softly did blow,
Round little Bethlehem
Long, long ago.

Sheep on the hillside lay
Whiter than snow;
Shepherds were watching them,
Long, long ago.

Then from the happy sky,
Angels bent low,

Singing their songs of joy,
Long, long ago.

For in a manger bed,
Cradled we know,
Christ came to Bethlehem
Long, long ago. (Author unknown)

National Curriculum cross-curricular reference

History and Geography are obvious links with the Christmas theme.
Both can be extended to consider such aspects as climate, clothes,
food and how these are linked to the Christmas traditions.

58   *Season of goodwill*

Introduction

When we think of Christmas in the British Isles it is usually with very
pleasant thoughts – our family and friends, people being kind and
generous to each other. We like to think of it as the season of
goodwill. For children in other parts of the world, it is sometimes
rather different.

Season of goodwill

Peru is a country in South America where there is desperate poverty.
A visit there shows how this affects young children.

In 1992 the school attendance figures in Lima, the capital, were
down by fifty per cent because so many children were taking time off
to earn money, or because their parents couldn't pay fees, or both.

Although by law children are not supposed to work until they are
fourteen, nobody seems to pay much attention to this rule. In Lima
the streets are full of children as young as six who are trying to earn
money. They do this in a number of ways.

Some sell small things like bubble gum or biros. One way of doing
this is to wait until cars stop at red lights and then rush up to them
and try and make a sale to their owners. This is obviously very
dangerous and there have been several accidents as a result.

Other children try to sell their services – they will clean anything
from shoes to cars for very small sums of money. Often when they go

home there is not enough food and their homes are broken-down, overcrowded shacks.

The children who do go to school don't have a particularly happy time either. School buildings are often in desperate need of repair and there are never enough books to go round. Worst of all, most state schools do not even have toilets.

Fortunately some people are trying to help. The Save the Children organisation is working hard in Peru to help these unfortunate children.

Information for the teacher

1 Save the Children, Mary Datchelor House, 17 Grove Lane, London SE5 8RD is a useful address to link with this assembly. This organisation estimates that there are some twenty-five million children in need through war, famine and poverty.
2 This concern with children would allow this material to be linked to an anniversary on 9th December. Arthur Pearson died on this date in 1921. As a philanthropist he raised funds for poor London children to enjoy outings into the countryside. He later founded St Dunstan's Home for the Blind.
3 This is an assembly obviously best suited for use with older children in the primary school. A Bible reading which might be used with it is Luke 21, 1–4:

> He looked up and saw the rich people dropping their gifts into the chest of the temple treasury; and he noticed a poor woman putting in two tiny coins. 'I tell you this,' he said, 'this poor widow has given more than any of them; for those others who have given had more than enough, but she, with less than enough, has given all she had to live on.'

Hymn suggestion

Come and Praise Vol 1 'Father hear the prayer we offer' No 48

Prayer

Father, Hear the prayer we offer – for those children who must work rather than go to school, and who suffer in so many other ways. As Christmas approaches give them hope, and let the kindness of those who wish to help be effective. Amen.

National Curriculum cross-curricular reference

This assembly obviously has strong Geography links – Peru, its location, climate, reasons for the difficulties described, etc. The latter could lead on to some CDT work in considering suitable materials for homes and how they might be used more effectively.

59   Kindness at Christmas

Introduction

Christmas is a time when people make special efforts to be kind to each other. There are many stories from all over the world which show this. Here is one of them.

Story

One Christmas Eve, long ago in Germany, a poor widow sat looking at her bare Christmas tree in her small hut. Her children were sound asleep in their beds, and she wished desperately that she could have afforded some decorations to put on the tree for them.

'It's no use,' she sighed, 'but at least I can make it clean and tidy.'

So she swept all round the tree, plumped up the branches and arranged it as attractively as she could. Then, wiping a tear from her tired eyes, she too fell asleep in the simple room.

No sooner was the widow asleep than a strange thing began to happen. Spiders appeared out of the woodwork and started to spin webs. These webs were draped over the Christmas tree from top to bottom and from side to side. Their work done, the spiders once more disappeared from view.

Then, an even stranger thing happened. For a moment it seemed that Jesus was actually in the hut with the poor woman and her children. Whilst this was happening, the tiny tree began to glow. Slowly the dull threads of the spiders' webs changed colour, until they became a beautiful, gleaming silver, glowing in the darkness of the hut.

As the first pale light of dawn shone through the hut window on Christmas morning, the widow and her children awoke. There were cries of delight as they saw the wonderful tree standing in all its glory in the corner.

'This is going to be a wonderful Christmas,' whispered the widow in amazement and joy.

From that time on, Christmas trees were often decorated with silver tinsel.

Information for the teacher

1 Another traditional German story on a similar theme is about a simple woodcutter and his family. Tired and poor, they hear a knock on their door on Christmas Eve.

Despite having barely enough for their own needs they welcome the boy who has knocked on the door. He is invited in and made welcome.

Next morning everybody is awakened by the singing of a choir of angels. The family has in fact given shelter to the Christ Child.

2 A useful book in this context is *Christmas is Coming* by Redvers Brandling (Simon & Schuster). It has a large section on Christmas stories, both fact and fiction.

Hymn suggestion

Come and Praise Vol 2 'I want to see your baby boy' No 117

Prayer

Dear God, At this and every Christmas help us to understand the true meaning of kindness. Amen.

National Curriculum cross-curricular reference

Art may be particularly well served by looking at some of the many beautiful pictures available which deal with Christmas. Bearing in mind the Attainment Target 1 comment that children should 'respond practically and imaginatively to the work of artists', then the work of Satoni Ichikawa in the beautiful book *Merry Christmas* (Heinemann) is just one example of material which could be used.

60 *Maria*

Introduction

Getting presents is fun – and so is giving them. This morning's story is about a little girl who had absolutely nothing to give, or so she thought.

Story

The weather was warm – as it usually was in this part of the world on Christmas Eve. It was just as well because the clothes Maria wore were little more than rags and could certainly not have kept her warm.

She stood on the edge of a graveyard watching people going to church on Christmas Eve. Each person who went into church carried a little box or parcel. Maria knew that these were presents which would be placed on a table next to the crib in the church.

'I wish I had a present I could give to the baby Jesus,' muttered Maria to herself.

At that moment a beautifully-dressed lady passed by. She was wearing a vivid red dress and she carried a gold-covered box in both hands. Maria looked at her shoes which gleamed with polish and were expensive and smart. Then the little girl looked down at her own feet. There were no shoes on them and they were dirty, with broken nails telling of many journeys through stony, dusty ground.

A tear slid down Maria's cheek and dropped on to one of her feet. It sparkled there for a minute in the moonlight and then was gone as quickly as it had come.

'I wish I had a present I could give to baby Jesus,' Maria murmured again.

It was then that Maria seemed to hear the voice in her head.

'Look behind you,' it said.

A little bit frightened, Maria turned and looked behind her. It wasn't a very pretty sight. The graveyard was not well cared-for and the gravestones were surrounded by a sea of weeds.

The little girl sighed. What was there to look at here? Then she heard the voice again.

'Pick some of the weeds.'

Looking at the tangle of dusty, miserable-looking weeds, she wondered why anybody would want to pick a bunch of them.

'Maria – pick a bunch of weeds.'

There was the voice in her head again. Turning her back on the stream of people going into church, the little girl knelt by the nearest gravestone and began to gather some of the weeds in her hands. When she had collected a large bunch she stood up and turned to face the church again.

'Now take the weeds into the church and put them beside the crib as a present for Jesus.'

For a moment Maria hesitated. How could she possibly put this pile of dirty, unwanted weeds beside all the other lovely presents? But somehow her feet seemed to move her towards the church door without her being able to stop them.

Soon she was passing through the great door. People looked curiously at her. Then she was moving down the long aisle towards the crib. As she did so a feeling of tremendous joy began to swell up within her. The other people in the church all seemed to be turning to stare at her, and as they did so their faces lit up with astonishment and wonder.

As Maria walked something incredibly beautiful was happening to the weeds. With each step she took, the leaves at the top of every weed stem turned into a brilliant, lovely red. When she reached the crib their vivid colour made all the other presents look quite drab.

Carefully Maria laid her flowers down. She still felt happy and joyful in a way she had never felt before. Not only had she been able to give a present to the baby Jesus, but it was also a present more beautiful than she could ever have dreamed of.

Information for the teacher

1 This story is based on the old Mexican folk tale of how the first poinsettias came into being. They are still sometimes known as fire flowers.

2 Some comment on other plants associated with Christmas might occur in connection with this story.

Holly featured in the Roman Festival of Saturnalia. People exchanged sprigs of it then because it symbolised eternal friendship. The fact that it bears fruit in winter was another reason why it was considered sacred.

Straw is significant in that in Middle Eastern countries at the time of Jesus' birth, mangers were made of clay or stone. The way of making them warmer and more comfortable was to line them with straw.

There are many legends associated with mistletoe. It was

thought at one time to cure illnesses, and if a soldier saw some mistletoe in a wood he would immediately cease from using his weapons for the rest of that day.

In the Norse legends, Loki used mistletoe to kill Baldur. After Baldur returned to life the gods agreed that mistletoe should never hurt anyone again. Thus it became the symbol of love.

Tree worship was pagan in origin but St Boniface is credited with being the person who told his followers that the fir tree would be 'the Christmas tree'. In the sixteenth century its church steeple shape was used by Martin Luther to display candles.

Queen Victoria's husband, Prince Albert, introduced the Christmas tree to England in 1841.

Hymn suggestion

Come and Praise Vol 2 'The holly and the ivy' No 119

Prayer

Dear God, Let us give thanks at Christmas for all the beautiful trees and plants of the world. Let us admire this beauty and value our natural world. Help us to care at all times for our environment. Amen.

National Curriculum cross-curricular reference

Science, in its environmental aspect, could be a natural follow-on from this story, particularly in the context of 'knowing that human activity may produce changes in the environment that can affect plants and animals'.

Locating and finding out something about Mexico, past and present, could embrace both History and Geography; and this story lends itself to evocative work in Art as well. For those with appropriate skills and instruments it could be dramatised with musical effects and background.

Section B

Class assemblies

This section contains a group of fully prepared *celebratory class assemblies*. There are suggestions linking them to significant times in the term.

Each assembly is detailed in terms of aims, materials required, calendar location, numbers involved, preparation, information and presentation.

Where there are playscripts for direct use with the children, these are provided in bigger print and can be photocopied.

One of the general aims of this section is to produce a detailed resource which requires the minimum of preparation but offers dramatic and thought-provoking assemblies.

1 *The ship of treasure*

Aim: to stimulate thoughts on *Harvest*, starting from an unusual viewpoint

Materials required: depends upon teacher's choice but basically painting materials and a tape recorder

Numbers involved: whole class participation, the children being divided into groups

Calendar location: September/October – harvest time

Information and preparation: The story is based on an old Dutch folk tale. In presenting it the class should be split into groups. Each group should have a narrator and should decide beforehand how they want to present their particular part of the story – dramatically, by sound effects, by pictures or overhead projection presentation, by readings.

The story can then develop in a varied and interesting way.

Presentation

Group 1

NARRATOR: This morning we are going to tell you the story of the ship, 'HENRIK 1.'

(*Group shows a picture of a Dutch sailing ship.*)

The 'Henrik 1' belonged to a Dutchman who owned a great fleet of ships. One day he said to the captain of the 'Henrik 1', 'I want you to bring me back a shipload of treasure, the best you can find'.

(*Picture of OWNER and CAPTAIN talking.*)

Group 2

NARRATOR: This order worried the captain, so he got all his crew together and spoke to them.

CAPTAIN: Men, we have been ordered to set sail and bring back a shipload of treasure. What shall we get?

1ST CREWMAN: Gold, skipper, gold – that's what we want. Gold, and lots of it.

2ND CREWMAN: Why just gold? What about silver and precious jewels?

3RD CREWMAN: Or rich silks and materials – easier to find and easy to sell for gold and silver.

CABIN BOY: I think you're all wrong. All of us here have been desperately hungry at one time or another. Food is the most precious cargo of all. I suggest we bring back a boatload of wheat.

1ST CREWMAN: He's got a point.

2ND CREWMAN: Hmm – I think you're right.

3RD CREWMAN: Let's vote.

NARRATOR: So the crew voted. They decided that a load of wheat would be the most precious cargo of all. The captain agreed and the 'Henrik 1' set sail.

Group 3

NARRATOR: The 'Henrik 1' was away a long time. When she returned she was low in the water, crammed with a cargo of the finest possible wheat. The captain went to see the owner. He was pleased with his work. But what happened? Listen carefully and you'll hear what they said to each other.
(*At this point a tape recording could be played. It could have been carefully prepared beforehand by Group 3 and would consist of the conversation between CAPTAIN and OWNER, with lots of 'sea-going' sound effects in the background.*)

OWNER: You're back – wonderful! What treasure have you brought?

CAPTAIN: The greatest treasure of all – food.

OWNER: Food? Food! What do you mean, food? I want to see gold, jewels, fine silks.

CAPTAIN: Well I'm sorry but you did tell me to bring back what I thought was the greatest treasure – and I know there are lots of hungry people in this town. When that wheat is planted and . . .

OWNER: Enough! Enough! You've betrayed me. Throw all that wheat into the sea – and consider yourself out of a job!

CAPTAIN: But think of the waste . . . all that food . . .

OWNER: No buts – do it.

Group 4

NARRATOR: And so all the wheat was thrown into the sea.
(*Picture of wheat being thrown overboard from the ship.*)
But not long after this a terrible storm wrecked all the shipowner's fleet.
(*Picture of storm wrecking ships.*)
Within weeks he was ruined and penniless. Now he too knew the meaning of real hunger. One day he took a long walk along the coast. After walking for many miles he was astonished to see a coastal strip of land covered in growing wheat – his crop had come home!
(*Picture of wheat growing in abundance.*)
At once the former ship owner was sorry, and glad. He was sorry for his stupidity in having had the wheat thrown overboard, but glad that it had been washed ashore like this. And so he sent a message to the poor people of the town, telling them where there was plenty of food. They came and harvested the wheat.
(*Picture of harvesting.*)
Then they took the ship owner, who they had hated for his greed, and made him welcome, fed him and looked after him.

Conclusion

The assembly might be concluded by the singing of the hymn 'I planted a seed' (*Come and Praise* Vol 2 No 134); and the teacher could say a final prayer:
Dear God, Help us to understand the message of this story. Teach us to appreciate that food is a treasure we cannot do without. Teach us to value it and never to waste it.
Let us remember too, this morning, those people for whom there is never enough food. Let us pray that more help can be given to them.
Thank you God, particularly at this time of year, for your harvest. Amen.

2   *Possessions*

Aim: to focus attention on important values
Materials required: two benches necessary to form the structure
   within which the assembly takes place
Numbers involved: whole class participation in hymn, possibly
   prayers; smaller groups required for reading and action
Calendar location: October/November
Information and preparation: One of the great Hindu festivals,
   Dashara, takes place in the Autumn (see Religious Notes for
   October).

The climax of the celebrations is Durga Puja, the final day of the
festival.

The main theme of the assembly which follows is that the great
goddess, Durga, always has time to listen to the problems of
individuals.

This assembly requires very little preparation and a very simple
arrangement of props makes the movement within the play easy to
organise. The presenting arrangement should be as illustrated.

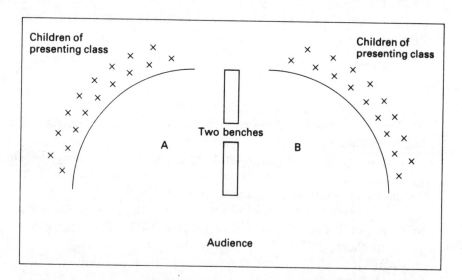

In the play Yashovarman has to move locations several times.
This can be done simply, by moving between the benches from A
to B on each occasion. This will create the image of moving from
one place to another.

Development of the assembly:
Characters: KING, YASHOVARMAN, DURGA, ARTHAVARMAN,
  BHOGAVARMAN, NARRATOR
Settings: The drama starts in the king's palace   (A)
  Moves to the temple of Durga   (B)
  To the home of Arthavarman   (A)
  To the home of Bhogavarman   (B)
  Back to the palace   (A)
Action: The action could be mimed to the reading of the various
  speakers. Yashovarman moves from A to B as appropriate.
Conclusion: At the end of the play there is a reading from the
  Upanishads and a prayer. These could be read by teacher or pupils.

Presentation

Yashovarman's discovery

NARRATOR: Yashovarman was a young man who lived in
  India. He worked at the palace of an enormously wealthy
  king . . .
KING: Yashovarman, I want you to deliver three messages for
  me. When you come back these ornaments need cleaning.
  After that come and see me – I have something else I want
  doing . . .
YASHOVARMAN: Your majesty . . .
KING: Yes?
YASHOVARMAN: Well . . . it's just that . . . I am never given
  anything for doing all my duties.
KING: Given anything? Indeed! You get food, don't you?
YASHOVARMAN: Yes, sir, but every day I see beautiful clothes,
  beautiful ornaments, this lovely palace – and I have nothing
  that I can even call my own.
KING: Get about your business. Remember you are a servant –
  here only to do my bidding.
YASHOVARMAN: Yes, sir.
NARRATOR: After this conversation with the king Yashovar-
  man became more miserable than ever. Eventually he could
  stand it no longer. Creeping out of the palace he journeyed
  up into the mountains to the temple of the great goddess
  Durga. Going inside he threw himself on to the floor.
(*Yashovarman moves from A to B.*)

YASHOVARMAN: May the great goddess Durga hear me. I will
lie here on the floor until one of two things happens: I will
either be here until I die, or the great goddess will grant me
one wish.

NARRATOR: For days the young man lay on the hard stone
floor. The goddess knew he was there of course and finally,
feeling sorry for him, she appeared.

DURGA: So, young man, you want me to grant you one wish.
What is it?

YASHOVARMAN: Majesty – I wish to have a great deal of
money so that I can be happy.

DURGA: I will grant you one wish, but you must choose –
money or happiness.

YASHOVARMAN: But there is no difference – with money you
are happy.

DURGA: Before you make your choice you must visit the
homes of two merchants, Arthavarman and Bhogavarman.
Then return and I will grant your wish.

YASHOVARMAN: Majesty.

(*Yashovarman bows low,* DURGA *disappears.*)

NARRATOR: And so Yashovarman came to the house of
Arthavarman.

(*Yashovarman moves from B to A.*)

YASHOVARMAN: What a fantastic place! This fellow must be
richer than the king I worked for. Look at the furniture and
look at how wonderfully the house is decorated. And the
jewels, they're everywhere!

ARTHAVARMAN: Can I help you, young man?

YASHOVARMAN: I'm sorry. My name is Yashovarman and I
was told to visit you. What a marvellous home you have
here. It's just wonderful.

ARTHAVARMAN: Umm – it's all right. Look, would you like
something to eat? (*Rather sourly*) There's a meal prepared
for us.

YASHOVARMAN: That sounds a very good idea.

ARTHAVARMAN: Come this way, then. Here it is.

YASHOVARMAN: But this is fantastic . . . There's biriani, and
fruit and nuts and . . . I've just never seen so much food in
one place before.

ARTHAVARMAN: Umm – well we always have the same here. Help yourself.

YASHOVARMAN: Aren't you going to join me?

ARTHAVARMAN: Well . . . only for a tiny bit. You see the doctor says I can't eat much because I've got a bad stomach. So I'll just have a tiny bit of food.

YASHOVARMAN: I'm sorry to hear you're not well.

ARTHAVARMAN: Well it's worry you know. Every night I lie awake worrying that I'm going to lose all my money the next day. So I can't sleep properly and I can't eat . . . aagh.

NARRATOR: That night Yashovarman heard Arthavarman tossing about in his bed – groaning with the discomfort of the pains in his stomach. The next morning he left the house of the rich merchant and went to visit one who was much poorer – Bhogavarman.

(*Yashovarman moves from A to B.*)

BHOGAVARMAN: Morning my friend, what can I do for you?

YASHOVARMAN: I've been told to come and visit you.

BHOGAVARMAN: In that case come in, come in. We'll have something to eat in a minute.

YASHOVARMAN: (*speaking hesitantly for he sees that Bhogavarman's house is very ordinary*) Err – nice place you've got here.

BHOGAVARMAN: Oh, it's nothing special but we find it comfortable enough. Come, let's eat.

YASHOVARMAN: Thank you, have you enough?

BHOGAVARMAN: Of course I've got enough, something shared is something enjoyed. Mind you, I'm very hungry so let's not waste any time getting on with it.

YASHOVARMAN: Do you enjoy your food?

BHOGAVARMAN: Enjoy it? I'll say I do. In fact I enjoy most things. Come on, it's not very fancy but it tastes good. Eat up.

YASHOVARMAN: Do you sleep well?

BHOGAVARMAN: Sleep well? What funny questions you ask, young fellow. Of course I sleep well. I work hard all day and I'm tired when I go to bed.

YASHOVARMAN: Yes . . . but . . . oh, it doesn't matter.

NARRATOR: And so Yashovarman ate and talked and stayed

with Bhogavarman, who was obviously nothing like as wealthy as Arthavarman, but who was equally obviously much happier. Soon the time came for Yashovarman to return to the temple of Durga.

(*Yashovarman moves from B to A.*)

DURGA: So, you've come back to claim your wish. What is it to be?

YASHOVARMAN: Your majesty, I was ignorant and foolish. Truly it is possible to be happy without money, but no amount of money can bring happiness.

DURGA: You have learned much in a short time, Yashovarman. Go, and enjoy a long, happy and contented life.

YASHOVARMAN: Thank you, majesty.

NARRATOR: We will now listen to the words of a Hindu prayer:

> God is the soul within my heart,
> Smaller than a grain of rice,
> Smaller than a grain of barley,
> Smaller than a mustard seed,
> Smaller than a grain of millet.
>
> God is the soul within my heart,
> Greater than the earth,
> Greater than the sky,
> Greater than the heavens,
> Greater than all the worlds.
>
> God is the soul within my heart.
> (From *The Upanishads*)

At this stage of the assembly the teacher may intervene with the following:

We can learn a great deal by finding out more about other people's beliefs. This morning's assembly reminds us that we all need help in our lives, and possessions and owning lots of things do not necessarily bring happiness. Let us end our assembly by singing a hymn which reminds us of these things.

The assembly can then end with 'The Family of Man' (*Come and Praise* Vol 1 No 69).

3 *Give and do not count the cost*

Aim: to emphasise the importance of being a good neighbour
Materials required: none
Numbers involved: whole class participation in hymn and prayers; smaller groups required for reading and/or action
Calendar location: any
Information and preparation: There are five pillars which every Muslim is expected to observe: Shahada – confession of the faith; Salat – prayer; Zakat – giving to the needy; Saum – fasting during Ramadan; Hajj – pilgrimage to Mecca.

   The assembly which follows highlights Zakat. It is in the form of a play reading and the scene is set by a narrator. Some introduction to the prophet Muhammad may be made by the teacher (if this is thought to be necessary).

Presentation

Characters: NARRATOR, MUHAMMAD, STRANGER, RACHID, HAMDAN, SERTAN, FATIMAH
NARRATOR: This morning we are going to hear the words of a Muslim prayer first of all:
   'That person is not a perfect Muslim who eats his fill and leaves his neighbour hungry.'
   These words were said by the prophet Muhammad and the play which follows shows just what they mean. Imagine that you can see into a mosque where Muhammad and some of his friends are sitting. They are talking when a stranger enters the building . . .
RACHID: Who is this fellow? He looks a bit the worse for wear.
STRANGER: Excuse me, I've just finished a really terrible journey and I haven't had a proper meal for days. I wonder if you could tell me where I might find something to eat?
MUHAMMAD: Come in, come in, my friend. I am certain you need look no further to find a good meal.
RACHID: Well I can't help. Sorry and all that, but I know we have (*hurriedly*) nothing to eat in our house.
HAMDAN: Same here. We never keep any extra food and

besides, if (*hurriedly*) you are tired after your long journey
it's a long way out to my house.

MUHAMMAD: What about you, Sertan?

SERTAN: Oh, certainly, our friend here must come to my house
for a meal. I'm sure we'll be able to find something! Let's go.

NARRATOR: So Sertan and the stranger left the mosque. When
they reached Sertan's house, he made the stranger comfortable and went to have a quiet word with his wife.

SERTAN: Fatimah – ah, there you are – we've got a visitor who
is going to join us for a meal tonight. Have we enough food?

FATIMAH: Oh, Sertan, why didn't you let me know sooner?
We've got barely enough for us and the children – barely
enough.

SERTAN: Oh dear, it's going to be embarrassing for our friend
to see how little we've got. He certainly won't eat heartily if
he sees we aren't doing the same.

FATIMAH: But what can we do?

SERTAN: I've got an idea. I'll go and talk to him while you feed
the children and put them to bed. Then we'll eat in the
darkness – I'll tell him we don't put the lights on in case they
wake the children up. That way he'll be able to have a decent
meal and he won't see that we aren't eating anything.

NARRATOR: So it was all arranged. The children were fed and
put to bed and Sertan, Fatimah and the stranger sat down in
only the faintest moonlight.

SERTAN: (*pretending to talk with his mouth full*) I hope you
won't mind us eating without lights, but you know what
children are – and we don't want them jumping about again.

STRANGER: It's quite all right, my friend. This meal is
wonderful. I must congratulate you on your cooking,
Fatimah.

FATIMAH: (*pretending to talk with her mouth full*) Thank you,
sir, but please, have some more rice, there's lots to eat up
here.

STRANGER: I couldn't eat another mouthful, thank you, and in
any case I must get back and see if my camels have been got
ready. I'm leaving at dawn. Thank you again so much. You
have been most kind. Now I must bid you farewell.

SERTAN and FATIMAH: Goodbye – and have a safe journey.

NARRATOR: And so the stranger left . . .

SERTAN: Well, my dear, I heard you say there was some rice left. As we haven't had any, I'm ready for it.

FATIMAH: Sorry, Sertan, I was just hoping our friend wouldn't want any more because he had all there was.

SERTAN: You mean . . .

FATIMAH: Never mind, think how much you'll enjoy eating again tomorrow!

SERTAN: You're right, and thank you, my dear, you fed our guest splendidly.

NARRATOR: So Sertan and Fatimah went hungrily but happily to bed. When Muhammad heard their story he said how pleased Allah must have been with their behaviour.

Now we are going to finish our assembly by listening to the words of some more Muslim sayings:

'People are not true believers unless they desire for others what they desire for themselves.'

'The best deeds are those done often, even if they are small.'

'Have mercy, good Lord, upon all those who, because of human unkindness, despair of human kindness.'

The service could then end with everyone singing: 'When I needed a neighbour' (*Come and Praise* Vol 1 No 65).

4 Birthdays

Aim: to emphasise the importance of our behaviour towards others, using birthdays as a starting point
Materials required: percussion, etc. for the singing of 'Happy Birthday', a Lowry print (*if one is readily available*), props as required for simple plays
Numbers involved: whole class participation
Calendar location: November
Information and preparation:
1 Guru Nanak was the founder of the Sikh religion. His birthday is celebrated in November. Great processions take place on the day preceding his birthday.
2 This assembly is unusual in that it offers several routes which may be followed. The choice here is one to be determined by teacher, children, location, materials available, etc.

The point at which the assembly becomes a specific, localised choice is marked * in the presentation script. Any of the possibilities described need to be prepared beforehand.

Presentation

The assembly begins with the presenting class singing and playing 'Happy Birthday to You' (see music provided). When this is finished the assembly could be developed by a series of readers.

READER 1: As you've guessed, our assembly this morning is about birthdays. Is there anybody here who has a birthday this week? (*pause for response*)

READER 2: There are some famous people who have birthdays in November.

READER 3: Yes, there's a famous painter called Lowry (*show a Lowry print here if possible*) . . . and then there's Prince Charles . . .

READER 4: And Nadia Comeneci, who was a great gymnast, and Sir Winston Churchill and . . .

READER 5: Grace Darling, who was a heroine who saved people from a shipwreck, and Lester Piggott, a famous jockey.

READER 6: And Guru Nanak, who was a very wise old man who always tried to help others.

READER 1: Listen to this story of Guru Nanak.

READER 2: A famous carpet maker called Nuri decided to give Guru Nanak a present of a really beautiful carpet.

READER 3: Guru Nanak saw the magnificent carpet and said to Nuri, 'You are so very kind, my friend, but I have absolutely everything I need. May I give your carpet to someone who really needs it?'

READER 4: Nuri said, 'Yes of course, master.'

READER 5: Guru Nanak took the carpet and placed it over a poor starving dog who was about to die unless he had something warm to cover him.

READER 6: This story shows us that when it is our birthday we are in the limelight – so this often gives us an opportunity to behave in a special way towards other people.

READER 1: Let us sing our 'Happy Birthday' song once again. (*All sing and play.*)

READER 1: Now we are going to present a play (or plays) and you will see how the person having the birthday has an opportunity to show an example in behaviour . . .

*At this stage in the assembly the play (or plays) which have been chosen, discussed and prepared beforehand could be presented. As with the Guru Nanak story these will contain a message in keeping with the assembly aim.

Some suggestions for development are as follows:

Scenario 1
It is Billy's birthday party:
PENNY: What a great birthday party. Pass the trifle, Billy, please.
BILLY: Here you are . . . oops . . . sorry!
PENNY: You've ruined my dress! You clumsy . . .
BILLY: Would you like to borrow my handkerchief?
PENNY: No. I'm leaving this stupid party right now.
   Continue.

Scenario 2
It is Izbel's birthday. A few days before the event her mother
has to go into hospital. The party is cancelled and mother is
very upset. What happens?

Scenario 3
It is Jaskeerath's birthday. Everybody gathers at his house for
the party. Then there is a knock at the door. When Jaskeerath
answers, he sees a strange creature there.
   'I am a Martian,' says the creature. 'I've heard it's your
birthday today. It's mine too, so I've come to earth to see what
it's like, and how people behave here.
   What happens?

Scenario 4
SALONI: John, you're the last to arrive for the party.
   Everybody else is here.
JOHN: I couldn't help being late. It's because I've got you a
   very special present. Look . . .
SALONI: It's . . . it's . . .
   Continue.

Scenario 5
Wayne is having a birthday party. Further up the street the
Robins family are living in a tent in their back garden because
their home has been damaged by fire.

Lee Robins is Wayne's age and Wayne doesn't like him or any of his family.

Just before Wayne's party, very heavy rain starts . . .

What happens?

5 *Let there be light*

Aim: to emphasise light – practical and symbolic – in all its contexts
Materials required: 1 For lighthouse demonstration: batteries, bulb,
   bulbholder, switch, crocodile clips, leads, o/h projector
   2 Diwali clay lamp, *diva*; menorah, or picture of one; Advent
   candles
   3 Whatever props seem necessary for the simple play
Numbers involved: whole class participation
Calendar location: November/December – could be used for a
   Diwali, Chanukah, St Lucy or Christmas presentation, if required
   (equally suitable for any or all of these)
Information and preparation: This assembly presentation is basically
in three parts:
   • a practical demonstration
   • some comment on light
   • a play
If more information is sought about lighthouses, the following
regional addresses are useful:
   Public Relations Officer, Trinity House Lighthouse Service, Trinity
House, Tower Hill, London EC3 (for England and Wales)
   Northern Lighthouse Board, 84 George Street, Edinburgh (for
Scotland)
   Commissions for Irish Lights, 16 Lower Pembroke Street, Dublin 2
(for Ireland)
   The model lighthouse will obviously need to have been constructed
(and tested!) before the assembly.

Presentation

The assembly could begin with a group of the presenting
children demonstrating the working of a model lighthouse.
   If an overhead projector is available then the following
information could be projected. Otherwise the same information could be displayed on a large piece of card.

How our lighthouse works

What we needed: batteries, bulb, bulbholder, switch, crocodile
   clips, fairly lengthy leads.
Technique: 1 The aim is to show how to make a flashing light.

The above materials should therefore be set up as illustrated, to show how this is done.

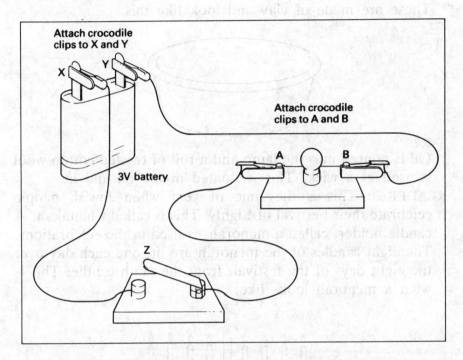

2 Once the circuit has been set up, pressing the switch Z will result in the bulb lighting up. Thus we can make our lighthouse flash when we want it to.

Some readers could then develop the assembly from this point.

READER 1: Guiding ships to safe anchorage was a problem as soon as they started to go on long voyages.

READER 2: Early attempts at doing this involved lighting fires. Unfortunately in bad weather rain put the fires out.

READER 3: The first great lighthouse was built in 300 BC. It was at Alexandria, stood 122 metres high and could be seen for miles around.

READER 4: There are over one hundred lighthouses around Great Britain and many of them are open to visitors.

READER 1: At this time of year lights are important for all sorts of reasons.

READER 2: At the great Hindu festival of Diwali, it is

remembered how Rama and Sita were guided home after their adventures by thousands of little lights called *divas*. These are made of clay and look like this:

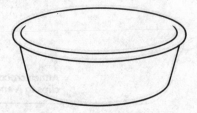

Oil is poured into the lamp and a roll of twisted cotton wool is used as a wick. This is floated in the oil and lit.

READER 3: This is the time of year when Jewish people celebrate their Festival of Lights. This is called Chanukah. A candle holder, called a menorah, is used in the celebrations. The eight candles of the menorah are lit, one each day over the eight days of the festival, from the ninth candle. This is what a menorah looks like:

READER 4: Christians light candles in Advent, one on each of the four Sundays before Christmas and the last one on Christmas Day itself. Advent candles look like this.

READER 1: You can see that light is very important for all sorts of reasons, as our play will remind us even further.

The three sons

(*This play can be mimed to the readings*)
Characters: NARRATOR, FATHER, IVAN, IGOR, PETER

NARRATOR: A very rich man was getting old and the time had come for him to choose one of his three sons to be head of the family after him.

FATHER: Now my boys, which of you is going to succeed me and care for the family? I am going to give you a test to see which of you is best suited to the job.

IVAN: What is the test, Father?

FATHER: We have a large storeroom in our house. I will give each of you one kopek. With that you must buy something to completely fill that room.

IGOR: One kopek – that's not much.

PETER: No, we'll have to buy cheaply at the market.

IVAN: Hmm, this is not going to be easy.

FATHER: You've got until the day after tomorrow. Then each of you can have his try.

NARRATOR: News of the test spread round the village. Who would win? On the morning of the test day several things happened.

IVAN: Come on you men, bring all that hay into the storeroom.

FATHER: What have all these men got, son?

IVAN: They are all carrying bundles of hay, Father. I bought it cheaply at the market and it will fill the storeroom.

FATHER: Hmm.

NARRATOR: The crowd gathered outside held their breath, as the storeroom was piled high with hay. But no matter how much was put in, there was still a little bit of space left.

FATHER: Well tried, Ivan; but you haven't succeeded. What about you, Igor?

IGOR: I'll do it, Father. Come on men – get busy with that sand. I got a great bargain at the market with this, Father.

FATHER: Hmm.

NARRATOR: Working as hard as they could, Igor's helpers carried and shovelled and piled the sand in the storeroom, but they couldn't get it right up to the roof. There was still some space left.

FATHER: Good try, Igor, but not good enough I'm afraid. Empty everything out so that Peter can have his try.

PETER: Thank you, Father.

FATHER: What – no men?

PETER: No, what I bought didn't even cost a kopek and I can certainly carry it myself.

FATHER: Oh?

IVAN and IGOR: What can he have got?

PETER: Would you all come into the storeroom with me please?

NARRATOR: Peter and his brothers and their father went into the storeroom. There Peter took a candle from his pocket and setting it down in the middle of the floor he lit it.

PETER: Would you close the windows and the blinds please?

FATHER: Do that please, Ivan and Igor.

PETER: There you are. The light fills the room.

NARRATOR: Gazing at the light-filled room Ivan and Igor agreed. Their father had found his successor.

The service could then end with a prayer and a hymn. The teacher might introduce the (adapted) prayer as being a well-known Hindu one which is used at Diwali:

> Lead us from bad things to good.
> From unreal things to real ones.
> From darkness to light.

The final hymn could be: 'From the darkness came light' (*Come and Praise* Vol 1 No 29).

(*Note*: The play in this assembly was adapted from a traditional Indian story)

6 Promises

Aim: to stimulate thought about important values at Christmas

Materials required: a simple doll, two more spectacular dolls, a 'magic' bottle, a party dress, party hats, crackers, parcels

Numbers involved: whole class participation, some specific speaking, acting/miming roles

Calendar location: Christmas

Information and preparation: This assembly is basically in three parts, all of which focus on the theme of promises. The first and third parts are combinations of words and music, whilst the second part is a play which can be acted or mimed to readings. The play is an adaptation of an old folk tale.

Presentation

The assembly may begin with everybody singing the carol: 'The Virgin Mary' (*Come and Praise* Vol 2 No 121). On completion of this the presenting group, who could be facing the audience in a previously-arranged grouping, speaks in unison:

'When Mary and Joseph came to Bethlehem nobody knew what a great event was about to take place.'

After this several individual speakers continue:

SPEAKER 1: But as the carol tells us . . .

SPEAKER 2: Some shepherds heard the wonderful news . . .

SPEAKER 3: As did some kings . . .

SPEAKER 4: The promise of Jesus's life had begun.

Everybody could then sing a second carol: 'I want to see your baby boy' (*Come and Praise* Vol 2 No 117).

Following this, a NARRATOR could continue the assembly:

NARRATOR: We have heard the word 'promise' mentioned. The dictionary tells us that a promise is something which 'raises our expectations'. We are now going to present a short play about promises.

At this point some party music could be played on the tape recorder or record player, and the play, which will have been prepared beforehand, could develop as follows:

NARRATOR: Our story takes place long before cars or buses existed. Most people walked to where they wanted to go. First of all we see a party – watch out for Elizabeth.
(*Enter children, obviously at a Christmas party, with hats, crackers, parcels in evidence*)

JOHN: This is a great party.

JENNY: Smashing.

ELIZABETH: It's a pity it's time to go home.

TANYEL: Yes but . . .

SERTAN: I know – but we are all going to get a present to take home.

EVERYBODY: Hurray!

MRS JOHNSON: You've all been very good children. Now I want to wish you all a merry Christmas, and give you a small present to take away with you. John.

JOHN: Thank you, Mrs Johnson.
(*JOHN receives a small parcel, as do the others in turn*)

MRS JOHNSON: Jenny.

JENNY: Thank you, Mrs Johnson.

MRS JOHNSON: Tanyel.

TANYEL: Thank you, Mrs Johnson.

MRS JOHNSON: Sertan.

SERTAN: Thank you, Mrs Johnson.

MRS JOHNSON: Elizabeth.

ELIZABETH: Thank you, Mrs Johnson.

NARRATOR: So the children all got a present to take home with them. We are going to follow Elizabeth.
(*The other children all move off, leaving ELIZABETH standing alone at the front. She slowly unwraps her present and reveals a very modest doll.*)

ELIZABETH: It's lovely! It's the best present I've ever had. I'd never part with this doll. I wouldn't swap it for anything. Well, I'd better be walking home, and it's such a long way.
(*ELIZABETH walks a 'long way'*)

ELIZABETH: I'm so tired. I just must have a rest.
(*Enter an old woman*)

OLD WOMAN: My child, you shouldn't be sitting here on such a cold snowy night. You'll catch cold.

ELIZABETH: I'm just having a rest, I've walked so far.

OLD WOMAN: Oh, I see. What's that you're carrying, by the way?

ELIZABETH: It's a doll. I've just got it from a party. Don't you think it's lovely?

OLD WOMAN: It's all right . . . but I tell you what . . . if I promise you two much bigger, better dolls, will you give me that one? Look . . .

(*The OLD WOMAN claps her hands and utters a 'magic' word as a boy enters carrying two much more elaborate dolls*)

ELIZABETH: They're lovely too, but I prefer to keep my doll, thank you, it's very special you see.

OLD WOMAN: Hmm. But what if I gave you a magic bottle? One you could drink from for the rest of your life and it would never, ever empty – look!

(*Another hand clap and 'magic' utterance from the OLD WOMAN and another boy brings in a spectacular-looking bottle*)

ELIZABETH: It would be a marvellous present, but I'd rather keep my doll. It really is very special.

OLD WOMAN: Ah, but I'm sure you'll change it for this.

(*The OLD WOMAN claps hands, etc. A beautiful party dress is brought on.*)

OLD WOMAN: Now look at this dress. It has magic qualities – it never needs washing and no matter how much you grow it will always be a perfect fit. It must be a good exchange for a little doll.

ELIZABETH: It really is lovely, but I wouldn't exchange my little doll for anything.

OLD WOMAN: How about *all* the things you see before you? I promise you, you can have them all in exchange for your doll.

ELIZABETH: Sorry.

OLD WOMAN: Well, I've got some bad news for you. Your mother is very, very ill and the only thing that can save her is a handful of this special snow that I am holding in my hand. Will you give me your doll for this handful of snow?

ELIZABETH: Oh, yes, yes, take it please – and help me to get home as quickly as possible through the snow. Please, please hurry!

OLD WOMAN: Calm yourself, my child. Here, take the snow and keep the doll. All is well now that you have the snow in your hand. The people who know you in their lives will be very fortunate indeed.

(*The OLD WOMAN and ELIZABETH move off in different directions*)

NARRATOR: Now let us return to Bethlehem, and that time of promise which was the first Christmas.

(*If it has been possible to arrange a tableau behind some curtains whilst the play has been going on, this should now be revealed – Mary, Joseph, shepherds, etc.*)

NARRATOR: Now let us all sing: 'Christmas time is here' (*Come and Praise* Vol 2 No 127).

Section C
Anniversaries, facts, fancies, anecdotes and religious notes

Many assemblies can be developed from the fertile ground suggested by the above title. This section aims to provide a selection of such starting material.

The autumn months

Introduction

Much of the information here will serve as source material for locally-developed assemblies. Where a particular event can be linked to an assembly (or assemblies) already detailed in this book, then there is an appropriate reference to aid teacher planning.

A note about the various calendars which govern the festivals of different faiths is important. *The Gregorian calendar*, which is solar-based and used in most western countries, enables most festivals related to this to be fixed. An exception is Easter, which is a movable feast. *The Jewish calendar* is lunar-based and to adjust it to the solar year an extra (embolismic) month is added seven times in each nineteen-year period. *The Islamic calendar* is lunar-based without adjustment, which means that Muslim festivals advance by some eleven to twelve days each year. More than one calendar has been in use in India.

The impact for teachers of these calendar fluctuations is that an annual plan of great religious festivals can only be accurately made by reference to the relevant current calendars. Otherwise it is a question of moving source material about as appropriate.

SEPTEMBER

1st   Feast Day of St Giles, patron saint of handicapped people. A day remembered in Ireland for the death of Patrick O'Bryen (1806). At 8 feet 5 inches in height, he was one of the tallest men who ever lived.

Supposedly the day in 1896 when chop suey was served for the first time in America by a Chinese chef.

Edgar Rice Burroughs, creator of Tarzan, was born in 1875.

2nd On this date in 1752 Britain adopted the Gregorian calendar. The Great Fire of London began in the bakery belonging to a man called Farryner, who lived in Pudding Lane. (*Link – Assembly 3*)

3rd Because the Gregorian calendar was adopted, eleven days were 'removed' from the calendar. This caused riots because people thought eleven days were being taken from their lives.

Louis Sullivan, the architect who designed skyscrapers, was born in 1856.

Sinking of the 'Delaware' in 1863. (*Link – Assemblies 3, 10*)

4th   In 1567 Queen Elizabeth I allowed two Flemish merchants to work in England, and teach Englishmen their skill of glass-making.

      In 1909 the first Boy Scout Rally was held in London.

5th   Count Barowloski died near Durham in 1837. He was ninety-six years old and had never grown to three feet high.

      St Laurence Justinian, the patron saint of Venice, died in 1455.

6th   The 'Mayflower' sailed from Plymouth in 1620. Seventy-four men and twenty-eight women were on board. (*Link – Assembly 2*)

7th   In 1533 Henry VIII's wife Anne Boleyn gave birth to a daughter – Elizabeth.

8th   In 695 a monk supposedly heard angels singing and when he asked why they were celebrating he was told that this was the anniversary of the birth of Mary, mother of Jesus.

9th   In 1835 the 'sport' of bear baiting was banned by parliament.

      In 1754 William Bligh, Captain of the 'Bounty', was born.

10th William the Conqueror died in 1087.

      Scape Goat Day: a traditional Jewish custom was that a goat was let lose in the desert on this day. This was the 'scape goat' and it carried with it all the sins of the people. (*Link – Assembly 6*)

11th Death of Roger Crab in 1680. (*Link – Assembly 2*)

      A famous quotation was supposedly written by Benjamin Franklin on this day in 1773: 'There was never a good war or a bad peace.'

12th John Alden, the last of the 'Mayflower' Pilgrim Fathers, died in 1687.

13th The *Catholic Annual* of this date in 1830 carried a health warning about eating only ripe, and moderate quantities of autumnal fruit at this time of the year. (*Link – Assembly 8*)

14th Holy Rood Day. *Rood* is another word for *cross* and traditionally on this day children were freed from school and work so that they could gather nuts.

      The actual cross on which Jesus was crucified was supposedly found by St Helena. To commemorate this, her son, Constantine, built a great church in Jerusalem and it was opened on this date in 335 with the ceremony of the Exaltation of the Holy Cross. The annual custom has endured.

      Robert Raikes, founder of Sunday Schools, was born in 1735.

15th The Liverpool–Manchester railway was opened in 1830.

      This was the date in ancient Rome when the Circensian Games were held annually. An imitation of the Greek Olympic Games, the main event was the pentathlon – leaping, wrestling, throwing, boxing and racing on foot and by chariot.

Battle of Britain Day, commemorating the RAF's victory in 1940. (*Link – Assembly 13*)

16th The German inventor of the thermometer, Gabriel Fahrenheit, was born in 1736.

17th The first person ever to be killed in an aeroplane accident died in 1908. This happened in America and his name was Thomas Selfridge. (*Link – Assembly 55*)

Sir Francis Chichester, solo round-the-world sailor, was born in 1901. (*Link – Assembly 7*)

18th Peter Sellers, one of Britain's funniest actors, was born in 1925.

The Emperor Domitian was a ruler of such cruelty that he had polished stones planted on all his walks. These acted like mirrors so that he could see if his many enemies were about to attack him. He was killed by his 'friends' on this date. (*Link – Assemblies 47, 51*)

Dr Johnson was born in 1709. (*Link – Assembly 11*)

19th Dr Barnardo died in 1905. (*Link – Assembly 1*)

Mickey Mouse featured in his first cartoon in 1928.

An old Derbyshire belief is that a storm on this date means that the winter will be mild.

George Cadbury, chocolate maker and philanthropist, was born in 1839.

20th Eton School was founded by Henry VI in 1440.

Muhammad changed the name of the city of Yathrib to Medina. (*Link – Class Assembly 3*)

Rahere, court jester and founder of St Bartholomew's hospital in London, died in 1144.

Jacob Grimm, fairytale writer, died in 1863.

21st This is St Matthew's Day. An ex-tax collector and disciple of Jesus, he died in the first century. By the time of his death his writings had become more prolific than any other gospel chronicle. It was said he used an angel's feather to write the first gospel, and his name is linked to many old sayings, for example, 'St Matthew's Day sends sap into the tree.' (*Link – Assembly 9*)

22nd This is the date on which, in 286, the Emperor Maximan ordered the death of one of his generals and an entire section of his army because they refused to give up their Christian beliefs. So died St Maurice and six thousand, six hundred soldiers. (*Link – Assembly 5*)

Michael Faraday, the scientist who invented the first dynamo to make electricity, was born in 1791.

23rd Today is St Thecla's Day. For refusing to give up her Christian belief, she was sentenced to be killed by wild beasts. They became calm in her presence, however, and wouldn't do her any injury. She died peacefully during the first century.

24th Traditionally this was the day on which harvesting began in medieval England:

Harvest home, harvest home,
We have ploughed, we have sowed,
We have reaped, we have mowed
We have brought home every load,
Hip, hip, hip, harvest home, hurrah!
(*Link – Assembly 8, Class Assembly 1*)

25th Samuel Pepys wrote in his diary in 1660 that this was the date on which he drank his first ever cup of tea. (*Link – Assembly 3*)

26th In 1580 Sir Francis Drake and his fleet returned to England after taking great treasure from Spain. (*Link – Class Assembly 1*)

The 'Queen Mary', then the world's greatest ship, was launched at Clydebank in 1934. A crowd of 200,000 watched King George V and Queen Mary perform the launching ceremony.

27th A woman was arrested for smoking a cigarette in a car in New York in 1905.

The world's first passenger railway (from Stockton to Darlington) opened in 1825.

28th Louis Pasteur died in 1885. He was the French scientist who introduced 'pasteurisation'.

This date is Michaelmas Eve, a time of nut-cracking amongst medieval church congregations, and one of those rare occasions when master and men were considered equal.

29th St Michael's Day, or Michaelmas Day. The Archangel Michael killed Lucifer the traitor angel and his feast day was very significant in the England of former years.

On this day rents were due and for those who couldn't pay, geese were often sent to landlords as presents in the hope that longer credit could be obtained.

There are many old sayings associated with the day, for example:

'The Michaelmas Daisy among dead weeds
Blooms for St Michael's valorous deeds.'

30th This was the date agricultural labourers (after 1351 and the Statute of Labourers) sought new jobs for the following year at market town fairs. (*Link – Assembly 15*)

The foundation stone of Nelson's Column was laid in 1840. In 1846 the first tooth extraction under anaesthetic was performed. (*Link – Assembly 14*)

Religious notes

Harvest Festival is usually celebrated in schools at the end of September and work in this book is aimed at this time.

September is also the month when the Hindu festival of Janam Ashtami could be considered. This festival celebrates the birth of Lord Krishna. The day before is one of fasting and prayer and a time when special sweets are put in images of Lord Krishna as a baby in a cradle.

Because of the many sides to Krishna's character – hero, people's champion, enjoyer of life – he is a very popular Hindu figure. As well as prayers, there are songs and plays about the great adventures of his life. The latter are told in the epic story, the *Mahabharata*.

The teachings of Lord Krishna are recorded in the *Bhagavad Gita*, which means 'Song of the Blessed Lord'. An example is:

'He who offers to me with devotion only a loaf, or a flower, or a fruit, or even a little water, this I accept from that yearning soul, because with a pure heart it was offered with love.' (9:26)

Jews observe Succoth, the Feast of the Tabernacles, at this time of the year. Similar to the Christian Harvest Festival, it is a time of family celebration in specially-created temporary buildings, usually set in gardens.

The Old Testament sets the guidelines for this festival:

'Thou shalt observe the Feast of the Tabernacles seven days after thou hast gathered in thy corn and wine – and thou shalt rejoice in thy feast, thou, and thy son, and thy daughter, and thy manservant, and thy maidservant, and the stranger.'

OCTOBER

1st   Traditionally this was the date on which the English pudding season started. These were filled with steak, leeks, mushrooms, spices and some were cooked for as long as sixteen hours. (*Link – Class Assembly 4*)

Paul Dukas ('The Sorcerer's Apprentice') was born in 1865. Lord Shaftesbury, social reformer, died in 1885.

2nd   Mahatma Gandhi, Indian leader, was born in 1869.

Aristotle died in 322 BC.

A curious custom takes place at Braughing in Hertfordshire on this date. Church bells are rung initially in a solemn manner, and then joyfully.

This is to commemorate Matthew Wall, a sixteenth-century farmer who was on the way to his funeral when the coffin was dropped. Wall, who had been mistaken for dead, recovered consciousness in the fall, and was released from the coffin.

3rd   In 1754, a French nobleman won a wager that he could ride from Fontainebleau to Paris in less than two hours. He completed the forty-two mile journey in just over one-and-a-half hours, but the horses he used died from overexertion. (*Link – Assembly 20*)

4th   St Francis of Assisi died in 1226. Up to the age of twenty-five Francis was a wastrel. A serious illness changed this. He became a Christian and, much to the annoyance of his rich father, gave away large sums of money to the needy. (*Link – Assembly 24*) He wore only the poorest of clothes and lived frugally. Impressed by his devotion, many people became followers. Known as Franciscans, they too practised self-denial.

5th   In 1930 the great British airship R101 crashed into a hillside at Beauvais, in France.

6th   Thor Heyerdahl, explorer and leader of the Kon-Tiki expedition, was born in 1914.

W K Kellogg, inventor of corn flakes, died in 1951.

7th   This was the date on which the famous diarist John Evelyn recorded a significant visit in 1644. This was to a galley in the harbour at Marseilles. Here he saw galley slaves double-chained about their waist and legs, in couples, and made fast to their seats '. . . commanded by cruel and imperious seamen'.

8th   In 622 the prophet Muhammad entered Medina on a camel. (*Link – Class Assembly 3*)

A strange duel took place in Paris on this date in 1361. A man called Macaire was suspected of having murdered another man called de Montidier. Unfortunately the only witness was de Montidier's dog. The king decided that a duel should be fought between dog and suspected murderer. During the course of this, so determined was the dog to seek retribution for its master's death, that Macaire confessed to the murder. (*Link – Assembly 12*)

9th   The famous district of Montmartre in Paris is particularly significant today. In 272 St Denis, patron saint of France and first Bishop of Paris, was beheaded for his beliefs. He is said to have carried his own head after the execution. The place where this occurred was called the 'mountain of the martyrs', or Montmartre.

Camille Saint-Saëns (composer of 'Carnival of the Animals') was born in 1835.

10th   Lord Nuffield, car manufacturer and philanthropist, was born in 1877. (*Link – Assembly 16*)

11th   Sir George William, founder of the YMCA, was born in 1821.

This is the day after which it is supposedly unlucky to gather blackberries. Thrown out of heaven by St Michael, Satan fell in a blackberry bush on 11th October and put a curse on the bush.

12th   Elizabeth Fry, reformer of English prisons, died in 1845. (*Link – Assembly 23*)

This is Christopher Columbus day in South America. In the USA it is celebrated on the second Monday in October.

13th   Margaret Thatcher, former Prime Minister, was born in 1925.

The Roman festival of Fontinalia – water worshipping – took place annually on this date.

14th   King Harold was killed at the Battle of Hastings in 1066.

The *Literary Digest* of 14th October 1899, carried some comment on the 'horseless carriage' saying that . . . 'it will never, of course, come into as common use as the bicycle.' (*Link – Assemblies 16, 20, 30*)

Martin Luther King was awarded the Nobel Peace Prize in 1964.

15th   P G Wodehouse, author and creator of Jeeves and Wooster, was born in 1881.

Florence Nightingale was appointed to organise the military hospital at Scutari in the Crimea in 1854.

16th   This was the date of John Brown's stand against slavery in the Battle of Harper's Ferry in 1859. Seizing the army base there, he thought that nearby slaves would rush to help. They didn't and he was executed. Slavery was only abolished in the USA after the Civil War.

'John Brown's body lies a-mouldering in the grave,
But his soul goes marching on.'

17th   This is St Audrey's Day. The daughter of an East Anglian king, Audrey was famous for her good works in the seventh century. (*Link – Assembly 17*)

18th　St Luke's Day. As one of the most talented of Jesus' followers, Luke was a practising doctor and artist as well as the writer of a gospel. He was crucified in the year 63 in Syria. (*Link – Assembly 26*)

19th　Jonathan Swift, author of *Gulliver's Travels*, died in 1745.

20th　Grace Darling, lifeboat heroine, died in 1842. In 1838, along with her father, she saved the lives of nine people from the disintegrating ship 'Forfarshire' off the coast of Northumberland. She was awarded several medals but was only twenty-seven when she died of consumption. (*Link – Assemblies 4, 10*)

　　　Christopher Wren, architect, was born in 1622. (*Link – Assembly 28*)

　　　In 1822 the first issue of *The Sunday Times* appeared. (*Link – Assembly 11*)

21st　Nelson was killed at the Battle of Trafalgar on this date in 1805. The battle lasted four hours and the admiral was killed by a musket bullet.

　　　Thomas Edison invented the light bulb in 1879. (*Link – Assembly 5*)

22nd　The first successful parachute jump was made from a balloon on this date in 1797. The event took place in Paris and the parachutist was Andres Jacques.

23rd　This is the birthday of Pele (1940), the only footballer ever to score a thousand goals in first class matches. (*Link – Assembly 19*)

24th　Cranberries were brought to England by voyagers returning from America in 1667. King Charles II was said to have liked them very much.

　　　United Nations Day since 1946.

25th　The Battle of Agincourt took place in 1415. Henry V's army of thirty thousand defeated one hundred thousand Frenchmen. In Shakespeare's *Henry V* the reference to this victory on St Crispin's Day is significant.

　　　St Crispin was martyred by the Emperor Maximilian in 287. He preached his beliefs during the day and earned his living by making shoes at night. Thus, apart from the literary references, he is also the patron saint of cobblers, and perhaps long-distance walkers because . . .

　　　Dear Saint, the saint of those who make good shoes,
　　　Thee for my patron saint I also choose;
　　　Where'er I walk in highway, trail or street,

Bring thou unblistered home my grateful feet.

In 1854 the Charge of the Light Brigade took place in the Crimean War. (*Link – Assembly 30*)

26th Igor Sikorsky, inventor of the helicopter, died in 1972.

The Football Association was founded in 1863.

27th Captain James Cook, the explorer, was born in 1728.

28th Alfred the Great died in 901.

The Statue of Liberty was unveiled in New York in 1886.

29th Sir Walter Raleigh, explorer and seaman, died in 1618.

30th A minor planet, Hermes, just missed a collision with the earth, which would have destroyed both, in 1937. (*Link – Assembly 27*)

Jean Henri Dunant, founder of the Red Cross, died in 1910.

31st The heathen festival of Hallowe'en was taken over by Christians for a threefold commemoration of Christian dead on All Hallows' Eve (31st) followed by All Hallows' Day and All Souls' Day.

Religious notes

The Jewish Festival of Rosh Hashanah takes place in the Jewish month of Tishri, which occurs in autumn.

This festival celebrates God's creation of the world; Abraham's sacrifice of a ram instead of his son; God as judge as well as creator; the need for atonement before God. Jewish years are calculated from Rosh Hashanah – thus it is also a new year celebration.

The Torah says: 'In the seventh month, on the first day of the month, shall be a solemn rest unto you, a memorial gathered with a blast of horns . . .'

The festival is started by the blowing of the sofar (ram's horn), which is a reminder of Abraham's sacrifice. Apples and bread are dipped in honey and eaten in the hope that this will bring a 'sweet' new year. New Year cards are sent to friends and relatives. These contain good wishes – *L'Shanah Torah Tikatevu.*

Despite the seriousness of the festival, it is not a time of gloom because it emphasises God's forgiveness and love. The festival builds up to Yom Kippur (The Day of Atonement), which is the holiest day of the Jewish year, and continuous prayers are said in the synagogue during this day.

Dashara is a Hindu festival which in some parts of India commemorates Rama's victory over Ravanna, whilst in others it is mainly concerned with the worship of the goddess Durga. The main day of the latter festival is Durga Puja. During the celebrations, clay statues of the goddess are made and treated with great respect and honour. After Durga Puja, the last day of the festival, they are symbolically thrown into the river – recognising the fact that the goddess will now have left these temporary homes. (*Link – Class Assembly 2*)

NOVEMBER

1st All Saints' Day. Saints are people of all ages and backgrounds who have achieved sainthood by being exceptional Christians. Two requirements were laid down for sainthood by Pope Innocent III in 1199: first, that the person concerned should have lived a life of inspiring virtue and second, performed miracles after his or her death. (*Link – Assembly 39*)

An interesting aside to All Saints' Day is that it was customary amongst better-off families in the sixteenth century to present an apostle's spoon to a child at his baptism. This spoon had the figure of the child's patron saint carved on its handle.

2nd This is the day when the Christian church remembers all its members who have died. A possible link is with Chinese Buddhists who also set aside a day for remembering – and helping – the dead. Of particular concern are homeless spirits without descendants, for whom large paper boats are burned to help them across the 'seas of hunger and thirst'.

This was the date in 1936 when the BBC's first television service began. (*Link – Assembly 43*)

3rd This being the month associated with saints, this date is the one on which St Winefride is remembered. Killed for her beliefs in the fifth century, a well of pure water is supposed to have sprung up on the spot where she died.

4th Felix Mendelssohn died in 1847. (*Link – Assembly 3*)

5th 'Now boys with squibs and crackers play,
And bonfires' blaze turns night to day.'
(*Poor Robin's Almanack*)

The plot to kill King James I in 1605 was hatched because of his supposedly unfair treatment of Catholics. Robert Catesby was the mastermind and Guy Fawkes the plotter designated to light the fuse to the gunpowder which would have blown up the Houses of Parliament.

A traitor betrayed the plot and the conspirators were all executed by 1606.

An interesting piece of trivia is that at St Peter's School in York, bonfires are lit there but never is a 'guy' burned. Guy Fawkes was an old boy of the school.

6th   In 1893 Peter Tchaikovsky, composer, died. (*Link – Assembly 35*)

7th   Marie Curie was born in 1867.

The River Thames flood barrier was completed in 1982. It took eight years to complete at a cost of four hundred and fifty million pounds.

8th   In 1922 Dr Barnard, the heart transplant surgeon, was born. (*Link – Assembly 44*)

9th   The first motor bike was ridden in 1885.

10th Thirteen-year-old Fritz Kreisler (born in Vienna) made his American debut as a concert violinist on this date in 1888. (*Link – Assembly 23*)

11th St Martin's Day. Martin, Bishop of Tours, died in 397. Perhaps best known for the story of the torn cloak (*Link – Assembly 39*), the fragment of the cloak given to the beggar was preserved as one of France's most holy relics.

This was also the date on which the Armistice was signed to end the First World War in 1918. Millions of men lost their lives in this conflict and as a permanent memorial to them the Menin Gate in Ypres, Belgium, was engraved with the names of fifty thousand men who have no known graves.

Traffic through this gate is halted every evening whilst the 'Last Post' is played on a bugle. (*Link – Assembly 40*)

12th King Canute died in 1305. The story of the limit of his powers (being unable to control the incoming tide) is still an effective one with children. (*Link – Assembly 41*)

13th Robert Louis Stevenson was born in 1850. (*Link – Assembly 35*)

14th Prince Charles was born in 1948.

Medzhid Agayer died in the USSR. He was one hundred and forty-three.

15th St Albert's Day. He died in Germany in 1280 and was considered one of the greatest scholars who had ever lived. (*Link – Assembly 35*)

16th The Suez Canal, one hundred miles long, was opened in 1869, after ten years of work.

Jack Sheppard, the infamous highwayman, was hanged in 1724.

17th One of Britain's most famous generals, Monty, or Field Marshall Viscount Montgomery of Alamein, was born in 1887.

18th This was the date, in 1963, on which the Dartford Road Tunnel was opened. This allows traffic to drive under the River Thames between Essex and Kent. (*Link – Assembly 16*)

19th In 1703 a prisoner died in the Bastille prison in France. He had been imprisoned for over twenty years, wore a velvet mask at all times and was mostly in solitary confinement. Later the subject of a famous book (*The Man in the Iron Mask* by Alexandre Dumas), the identity of the prisoner was shrouded in mystery. One supposition was that he was a criminal who looked so much like the king of France that he had to be masked.

20th Princess Elizabeth (now Queen Elizabeth II) was married in 1947.

21st The balloon designed by the Montgolfier brothers first flew in 1783. It attained a height of three thousand feet.

'Schinderhannes' died in 1803. He was the German Robin Hood.

22nd St Cecilia's Day. The patron saint of music, Cecilia was martyred in 230. (*Link – Assemblies 33, 53*)

The SOS call sign was adopted internationally: 'Mayday' comes from *m'aidez* (French for 'Help me'). (*Link – Assembly 41*)

23rd St Clement's Day. Clement was an early Pope who was put to death by being thrown into the sea tied to an anchor. Because anchors were made by blacksmiths, he became their patron saint.

24th In 1815 Grace Darling, heroine of the famous sea rescue, was born.

25th St Catherine's Day. Catherine was a fourth-century martyr.

In 1823 the first pier was opened – Brighton.

8am, 25/11/1872 was the last entry in the log book of the 'Marie Celeste', a ship found sailing in the Atlantic with no one on board.

26th The first Thanksgiving Day was held in the USA on this date in 1789. The original cause for Thanksgiving was the harvesting of the first crops by the Pilgrim Fathers in 1621. (*Link – Class Assembly 1*)

27th The first policewomen (Misses Allen and Harburn) started their duties in Grantham in 1914.

28th Enid Blyton died in 1968. Her books for children have sold over fifty million copies and have been translated into one hundred and sixty-five languages.

29th Concorde first flew in 1969. The agreement for its English–French joint development was signed on this date in 1962.

30th St Andrew's Day. The brother of Peter, Andrew was a

missionary in the Middle East until his crucifixion on this date in 70 AD.

There is an interesting 'weather saying' associated with this date: 'As November, so is the following March.'

Religious notes

One of the movable feasts which occurs in this month is Guru Nanak's birthday. Class Assembly 4 provides more detail of this occasion.

Chanukah, the Jewish Festival of Light, and a celebration often linked with Diwali and Christmas in primary school RE themes, also occurs at this time of the year. Class Assembly 5 refers to all three.

From a Christian viewpoint, the significance of All Saints' Day has already been mentioned and, at the end of the month, thoughts of Christmas are stirred by the arrival of Advent. This begins on the nearest Sunday to 30th November.

Advent Sunday is the beginning of the Christian church's year, except in the Greek church where it begins on 11th November, St Martin's Day.

DECEMBER

1st   St Eligius, a French Bishop, died in 659. He is memorable because he is the patron saint of so many groups of people . . . goldsmiths, blacksmiths, miners, locksmiths, clock makers, carriage makers, tool makers, cab drivers, farmers and jockeys!

2nd   The rebuilt St Paul's Cathedral was dedicated in 1697. (*Link – Assembly 28*)

3rd   1962 was one of the worst winters ever recorded in England. On this date fog paralysed London for four days and one hundred and six people died as a consequence. (*Link – Assemblies 45, 56*)

4th   In 1957 severe fog also contributed to a railway accident at Lewisham, in south London, in which ninety people were killed. (*Link – Assembly 44*)

5th   Mozart died on this date in 1791 at the age of thirty-six. Ironically his last composition was a Requiem Mass. (*Link – Assemblies 33, 53*)

6th   This is the Feast Day of St Nicholas, Bishop of Myra, patron saint of Russia and sailors, who died in 342. Renowned for his wisdom and generosity, Nicholas has become a figure closely associated with Santa Claus and Father Christmas.

The reason for his connection with sailors is that in 1807 some Italian seamen from Bari brought his remains back from Myra and lodged them in a church in Bari. (*Link – Assembly 57*)

7th On the Sunday morning of this date in 1941, Japanese aircraft from six aircraft carriers attacked the United States naval fleet at Pearl Harbour. Nineteen ships were sunk or badly damaged and over two thousand men were killed. (*Link – Assembly 50*)

8th Horace, the Roman poet, was born on this day in 65 BC. Greatly admired during his lifetime, many of his sayings are ideal assembly starters.

> 'No lot is in all respects happy.'
> 'Once a word has been allowed to escape it cannot be recalled.'
> 'When your neighbour's wall is on fire it becomes your business.'
> 'Seize today, and put as little trust as you can in tomorrow.'
> (*Link – Assembly 11*)

9th The first Christmas card was created on this date in England in 1842. (*Link – Assemblies 58, 59*)

Arthur Pearson died in 1921. He founded St Dunstan's Home for the Blind. (*Link – Assemblies 12, 34*)

10th In 1959 the Crowther Report recommended the raising of the school leaving age to 16 in England.

Alfred Nobel, the Swedish engineer who founded the Nobel prizes, died in 1896.

The Nobel prizes are awarded annually for achievements in physics, chemistry, medicine, literature, and service to the cause of peace. (*Link – Assembly 40*)

This date is Human Rights Day.

11th Hector Berlioz, the French composer, was born in 1757.

12th This was the date of Marconi's first transatlantic radio message in 1901. (*Link – Assembly 30*)

Robert Browning, author of 'The Pied Piper', a valuable assembly resource, died in 1889.

13th St Lucy's Day. A native of Syracuse, St Lucy was martyred in 304. She is particularly remembered in Sweden every year in a Festival of Lights, symbolic of her aid to early Christians. (*Link – Class Assembly 5*)

14th In 1918 women voted for the first time in a British general election.

15th Alexandre Eiffel, designer of the Eiffel Tower, was born in 1832. The tower in Paris is three hundred metres high.

16th Ludwig van Beethoven was born in 1770.

Wilhelm Grimm (one of the Grimm brothers) died in 1859. (*Link – Assembly 38*)

Camille Saint-Saëns, French composer of 'Carnival of the Animals', died in 1921.

17th In 1903 Orville Wright made the first aeroplane flight, near Kittyhawk in North Carolina, USA. He was aloft for twelve seconds and covered a distance of about forty metres. (*Link – Assembly 55*)

18th In 1865 slavery in the USA was abolished.

19th This was the date in 1981 when the tragedy of the lifeboat from Mousehole in Cornwall occurred. Trying to rescue survivors from the freighter 'Union Star', the lifeboat was fighting conditions of eighty-knot winds and twenty-metre-high waves when it sank. (*Link – Assemblies 4, 10*)

20th A fish caught off Madagascar in 1952 was recognised as being of a prehistoric species, a coelacanth.

21st St Thomas's Day. Thomas spread the gospel in the Middle East and India before dying in the first century. He is the patron saint of builders.

22nd Beatrix Potter (creator of *Peter Rabbit*) died in 1943.

George Eliot died in 1880. The plot of her novel *Silas Marner* contains some parts very well suited for assembly material. 'George Eliot' was in fact Mary Ann Evans.

This was also the date when 70mph speed limits were introduced on British roads in 1965. (*Link – Assembly 16*)

23rd Christmas Island was discovered by Captain Cook in 1777.

24th In 1933 the British Museum acquired the *Codex Sinaiticus*, an ancient manuscript of the Bible, written in the fourth century.

There is an ancient legend that on Christmas Eve the cock crows all night, thus keeping all evil at bay. (*Link – Assembly 48*)

25th The Queen's Christmas Broadcast was televised for the first time in 1957.

A useful quotation for Christmas Day comes from *Sketches by Boz* by Charles Dickens: 'There seems a magic in the very name of Christmas. Petty jealousies and discords are forgotten . . . would that Christmas lasted the whole year through.'

26th Boxing Day derives its name from the time when church poor boxes were opened on this date so that their contents could be distributed to the needy.

This is also St Stephen's Day. Stephen was the Christian church's first martyr, being stoned to death in 33 AD.

27th St John's Day. John was the last of the original disciples to die – in Ephesus in about 100 AD.

28th This was the night of the Tay Bridge disaster in 1879. The bridge collapsed in a storm as a train was passing over it. Seventy-five people died. (*Link – Assembly 52*)

29th The man who invented the raincoat was born on this date in 1776. His name was William Macintosh.

30th In the severe winter of 1962 this was the day on which the worst snowstorm since 1881 hit England. (*Link – Assemblies 45, 56*)

Rudyard Kipling was born in 1865. He won the Nobel Prize for Literature in 1907. (*Link – Assembly 35*)

31st The chimes of Big Ben bringing in the New Year were first broadcast in 1923.

Apart from being Hogmanay in Scotland, it is also a Hindu festival and the Shinto festival of Joya No Kane. Bells are rung at this time to give thanks for the good things of the past year and to prepare for the coming year.

Religious notes

Bodhi Day (Mahayana) is a movable feast in December when Buddhists celebrate the Buddha's enlightenment, as he reflected sitting under a Bodhi tree. 'Buddha' means 'the enlightened one' and the experience took place over two thousand five hundred years ago. (*Link – Assembly 48*)

Chanukah, the Jewish Festival of Lights, is also a November–December movable feast (see *Class Assembly 5* – 'Let there be light').

Christmas Day on the 25th of the month was not established until the time when Julius I was Bishop of Rome (337–352). Julius fixed this as the date, after various Christian communities had celebrated the birth on dates as diverse as 6th January and 29th March, with others in between.

Section D
Assemblies linked by theme

This section seeks to aid teachers who wish to present a number of assemblies linked by *themes* which are popular ones in a primary school and RE context. No assembly story from the book has been used more than three times in the groupings which follow. The assemblies are shown by their numbers and title.

ANIMALS

Class assemblies:

CONCERN

Class assemblies:

COURAGE

ENVIRONMENT

Section E
The stories

This section classifies the stories according to source categories – *folk, original or contemporary, religious, true* – for teachers who wish to use them in groupings of this nature. The assemblies are shown by their numbers and titles.

FOLK STORIES, MYTHS, LEGENDS

6   I'm sorry
11 For good and evil
17 A tale of two sisters
21 Learning a lesson
23 Honesty
24 The rich and the poor
31 The friend
35 Know your strengths
38 Not so useless
42 A long tongue makes for a short life
46 Giving
47 You go first
50 Tough?
51 Justice is done
54 What's in a carol?
59 Kindness at Christmas
60 Maria

Class assemblies:

1   The ship of treasure
6   Promises

ORIGINAL OR CONTEMPORARY STORIES

1   She's new
2   Being different
14 Open wide
15 At the fair
18 Mums
19 What is it called?
22 One autumn afternoon
34 John and Errol
43 The star
44 How can I help?

RELIGIOUS STORIES

5   Laurence
9   What do we see?
25 A father's choice
29 Akiba
32 Happiness
36 The determined friends
39 The beggar
48 *Stop!*

Class assemblies:

2   Possessions
3   Give and do not count the cost
4   Birthdays
5   Let there be light

TRUE STORIES

Section F
National Curriculum
cross-references

This section is intended as a guide for teachers who wish to integrate these assemblies into other areas of the National Curriculum. The assemblies are shown by their number and title, listed under the appropriate subject heading (subjects in alphabetical order).

ART

8   This month (September)
18 Mums
20 Saved by a horse
27 This month (October)
35 Know your strengths
48 *Stop!*
49 This month (December)
59 Kindness at Christmas

CRAFT, DESIGN, TECHNOLOGY (CDT)

7   Marooned
10 A woman at sea
13 At the fair
23 Honesty
36 The determined friends
39 The beggar
52 The Tom Eadie story
58 Season of goodwill

ENGLISH

3   Keeping a diary
5   Laurence
6   I'm sorry
7   Marooned
11 For good and evil . . .
14 Open wide
16 On the roads
17 A tale of two sisters
18 Mums
19 What is it called?
21 Learning a lesson
22 One autumn afternoon
23 Honesty
24 A father's choice
25 Confucius
30 Sending a message
34 John and Errol
35 Know your strengths
37 This month (November)
38 Not so useless . . .
41 A life-saving swim
42 A long tongue makes for a short life
43 The star
44 How can I help?
47 You go first
49 This month (December)
50 Tough?
51 Justice is done

Section G
Resources

Addresses

For specially produced material there are some addresses which are essential.

One of these is: *Christian Education Movement*, Royal Buildings, Victoria Street, Derby DE1 1GW.

By subscribing to the Christian Education Movement, schools receive a termly mailing of material which is always useful for RE, and sometimes specifically aimed at assemblies.

The annual journal of the *SHAP Working Party on World Religions in Education* is another most valuable source, if only for the fact that it gives precise dates for every religious festival in that particular year. Teachers already familiar with the problem of movable feasts will appreciate this annual information. The address here is:

The National Society's RE Centre, 23 Kensington Square, London W8 5HN.

SHAP also offers a free information service to teachers via:

Vida Barnett, 81 St Mary's Road, Huyton, Merseyside L36 5SR.

SAEs are welcomed with enquiries, as they are when contacting the following useful addresses.

Two addresses for specific help for topics related to Hinduism:

Hindu Centre, 39 Grafton Terrace, London NW5

ISCON Educational Services, Bhakti Vedanta Manor, Letchmore, Herts. WD2 8ED.

A useful source for all aspects of Islam:

IQRA Trust, 24 Culross Street, London W1Y 3HE.

Jewish Education Bureau, 8 Westcombe Avenue, Leeds L58 2BS (This office supplies materials and advice concerning Jewish features).

Other useful addresses:

Independent Publishing Company, 38 Kennington Lane, London SE11. They publish a large selection of books, posters and cards relating particularly to South-East Asian countries.

Save the Children, 17 Grove Lane, London SE5 8RD. The magazines are a constant source of very good assembly stories.

Books and stories

One of the difficulties of recommending books is that, particularly in recent years, titles have not only gone out of print but have also changed publishers at a bewildering rate.

The wise teacher, therefore, will seek to build up a range in two areas. The first of these would be the background information type of book, including material like *Celebrations*, a series of booklets by Maurice Lynch (Ginn).

Festival, a series of booklets by Olivia Bennett (Commonwealth Institute and Macmillan); *Festivals and Saints' Days* by V. Green (Blandford); Black's *Bible Dictionary* (A.C. Black) are other most useful sources.

The second collection will consist of folk tales which often produce marvellous assembly material. New anthologies appear with great regularity and should always be examined carefully. Old favourites like *Anansi*, the *Hodja*, *Brer Rabbit* and Aesop's *Fables* are suitable for many re-tellings and adaptations.

A very good way to find out about new and useful books in this field is to subscribe to *Books for Keeps*, a magazine of children's books (6 Brightfield Road, Lee, London SE12 8QF).

Newspapers provide an endless supply of stimulating true stories, and the advantage of local newspapers is that they often have appropriate stories which have taken place in settings familiar to the children.

Teachers should not neglect Asian-owned newsagencies in certain areas either. These are useful sources for items such as Diwali cards and Hindu legends in comic strip form.

Finally, with regard to books, the BBC's *Come and Praise* anthologies are the source for all the hymns recommended in this book. It would be hard to better this series for primary hymns.

Other Musical Resources

With regard to musical material which can be used in school, there are many new and exciting publications available. In the context of special occasions related to this book, examples are:

Christmas

'The late wise man' by Dennis O'Gorman and Barry Hart (based on the old Russian folk tale of Artaban – suitable for juniors);
'The Christmas Farm' by O'Gorman and Hart

(a St Francis and animals and Christmas celebration – suitable for infants);

'Star of Wonder' by Barry Hart
(a fallen star is found in the street by a group of children and what happens next – suitable for infants/lower juniors);

'Around the world to Bethlehem' by O'Gorman and Hart
(a magic carpet collects children from around the world to travel to Bethlehem – suitable for infants/juniors).

All this material can be obtained from Fountain Publications, 108 Longlands Road, Sidcup, Kent DA15 7LF.

For a selection of slightly more unusual carols – in unison, two or more parts, in rounds, with easy arrangements – the Oxford University Press Music Department, Walton Street, Oxford OX2 6DP has a very good choice. For example, 'So gentle the donkey', 'Rejoice and be merry', 'Carol of the children', 'Donkey carol', 'Jesus child', 'Nativity carol', 'Star carol'.

Other festivals

From the same publishers 'Festivals' by Jean Gilbert is a useful anthology to use in conjunction with much of the material in this book. Suggestions for songs and musical activities relate to Harvest, Succoth, Diwali, Chanukah and Christmas – all autumnal celebratory occasions.